The
Philosophy
of History

by John William Miller

The Paradox of Cause

The Definition of the Thing

The Philosophy of History

The Midworld of Symbols and Functioning Objects

In Defense of the Psychological

The Philosophy of History

with Reflections and Aphorisms

John William Miller

W · W · Norton & Company

NEW YORK   LONDON

First published as a Norton paperback 1982; reissued 2000

Copyright © 1981 by W. W. Norton & Company, Inc.

Printed in the United States of America

Library of Congress Cataloging in Publication Data
Miller, John William.
    The philosophy of history with reflections and
aphorisms.
    1. History—Philosophy,   I. Title.
D16.8.M674   1981   901   80-29179
ISBN 0-393-30060-9

W. W. Norton & Company, Inc.
500 Fifth Avenue, New York, N.Y. 10110
W. W. Norton & Company Ltd.
10 Coptic Street, London WC1A 1PU

1 2 3 4 5 6 7 8 9 0

Contents

Publisher's Note

With a very few exceptions, the essays in this volume, though written with publication in mind, were not finally revised by the author. Several of them are excerpts from letters written to friends or students. The editing that has been done has been largely in the direction of eliminating repetition and personal references. The originals of both essays and letters are available for study in the Williams College Library.

Preface

The purpose of this book is to examine the experiences that suggest and authorize history.

History deals with the past, and a concern with things past is by no means to be taken for granted. Many persons appear far more closely engaged with the excitements of the present, or with the possibilities of the future, than with the irrevocable past. An interest in the past may represent nothing more than a personal peculiarity or private fancy, as if one might prefer to play cards or plant roses rather than make acquaintance with the figures, events, or outlooks of yesterday.

On the other hand, there seems always to have been a yesterday. Prior to the histories of document and record there were mythologies. The Greek pantheon does not begin with Zeus, but rather reaches back to his father Cronus and his grandfather Uranus. The Bible story opens on scenes never beheld by human eye, telling of creation itself, for both man and nature. Nor is that the whole account: in the revolt of angels, human affairs find meaning and explanation in the most distant spheres of being. To view these projections of earthly life as imaginative inventions may be correct enough. But the freest imagination reflects a need or urgency not yet satisfied by matter of fact or cautious theory.

Topics here will include the appeal of the ahistoric, the sense of time, causes in history, judgment in history, whether history is like memory, reason in history, and much else. A second theme, and the most original, will deal with symbols, the artifact, the midworld. This answers the question of the sort of knowledge that is found in history or any of the humanities. This is a good idea, so far as I can tell.

All I can do with the theme is tell a story. I can't argue. Nobody is just plain wrong. To keep the story-telling mood is hard for me. The story *contains* argument but is not contentious in itself. It can't prove anything; it can only *show* something. If one has new wine, one needs a new bottle. The very ways of being right or wrong change with one's views of peril or advance. Philosophy has to *be* universal, not seek *the* universal. It has to be individual, yet must show also that in this the human universal occurs.

The
Philosophy
of History

1

The Utility of Historical Study

History is one of the modes of learning from experiences. The most important factor in learning is the ability to say what one's experience was about. Unless one knows at least so much, one can hardly go on to say that it was a partial or mistaken experience. To learn is to fall back upon an assumed certainty in order to allow for its modification by addition or correction.

From the village where I live anyone can see a large horizontal ledge along the south face of East Mountain, but only those with some interest in geology can identify that ledge as the shore line of a former glacial lake called Lake Bascom. Anyone can see the river in the valley, the adjacent mass of the hill, and the horizontal ledge, but experience may, and usually does, end with these discrete impressions. The geologist identifies what he sees. He can, and does, ask questions about his impressions. He has opinions and can correct them. This process is what we mean by learning. The geologist falls back on a belief that vast changes have taken place in the earth's crust, changes that are duly caused, capable of exhibiting reason in nature, the illustration and embodiment of its laws and its uniformities. To learn is to find meaning in data and deeds, a meaning that occurs apropos of some assumed reality in which one is concerned. There is no evidence for one's impressions; one simply has them. The question of evidence, of knowledge or learning, occurs apropos of some assumed real situation, conceptual and imaginative, in which one has a concern.

Interest by itself does not account for learning. While it is necessary, it is not sufficient. Interest is vacillating. A person's interests are his own affair. But scientific learning is not to be avoided or pursued at one's caprice. There is no harm in not being interested in golf. Perhaps one plays tennis instead. But a different impression is created when there is no interest in nature. To have no interest in art is to invite an assessment not of one's knowledge alone, but of one's personality. These considerations hold for all the organized modes of learning or of experience. One can hardly altogether disavow politics or religion or economics, as one would bird-viewing or stamp collecting. One can leave the birds alone, and hunt the many varieties of aster or goldenrod, even sea shells. But the organized modes of knowledge exert a compulsion that disregards subjective interest. They represent no accident, no caprice or private preference, but rather the various loci of a reality that breaks in upon all men. Even if one is no economist one feels that somebody has to be. But one does not feel an analogous imperative to see that somebody plays golf. Not that one feels any objection to golf. Some golf courses are lovely, and they facilitate exercise and sociability. But so does a tennis court or a croquet lawn. One wants everyone to play, but not necessarily golf. One wants everyone to learn something, and necessarily some should learn economics.

History is one of the modes of learning that no one can avoid. It is an odd sort of knowledge, being concerned only with acts, and with the past. Perhaps we study history in order to avoid some of the practical mistakes made by others. If that is the case, we seem to be taking for granted that all men share the same interests and that they have tried to implement them. History, then, would be a general school, the record of what men have learned by way of accomplishing their purposes. In so far as one's interests are not those of other people, they have nothing to teach one. The farmer does not, as a rule, study navigation or the locations of reefs and shoals off the Carolinas. There is an extensive lore in falconry, but the modern individual is much more likely to fly an airplane than a falcon. In fact, one has to look in the dictionary for the meaning of the very words used in the handling of hawks. Certainly there is no objection to hunting with hawks, but it is so rare a sport that anyone who pursues it is very likely to find himself in the newspapers or even the *National Geographic* magazine. Similar considerations apply to many skills, once common enough, but now forgotten or treated as hobbies. There are a few people who practice archery, but most hunters use guns. In many parts of the world oxen are used as draft animals, but the motor tractor seems to receive a quick welcome. Hardly anybody can nowadays tell the age of a horse, and our children do not understand why one should not look a gift-horse in the mouth. A great deal of the past is forgotten because it has become irrelevant to modern needs.

Not only are past skills and learning no longer useful, but even present skills do not interest all of us. We are specialists, and have, individually, few skills and but limited learning. The carpenter is no linotype operator. He is not concerned with a great variety of present skills, not to mention those of the past. People with skill are not necessarily informed about the past, its triumphs and errors, but frequently use only present means for present ends. This advancement without repetition of past operations and errors is part of our "social heredity," but it is not history, where time is of the essence.

In a practical age one may wonder about the utility of historical study. There is nothing to be done about the past. We can't change it. Would it not, then, be more sensible to give our time and attention to present emergencies or to future hopes? An invention, a reform, or a new theory draws part of its prestige from its novelty, as if the present always needed to own force and originality. The past can easily seem only "a bucket of ashes," offering no warmth and no utility to the present. Even conservatives come to rest in what was once a revision, a turning away from the past. They stop with the Constitution of 1787, with the Athens of Pericles, or with Moses on Sinai. They rarely base themselves on the Egyptians or Sumerians or on more remote pastoral barbarians. Corydon and Phyllis weave enchantment only to those who no longer roam the steppes with their flocks and herds.

As utility, the past becomes our servant, and as the opportunity for display, it becomes our victim. Sometimes, too, we judge it and thank God that we are not as the rest of men. Still, men did once warm themselves over the fuel that is now but ashes. They too had their lives; they spoke and acted. Herodotus, the father of history, reminds us that the past is a piety: "Herodotus of Halicarnassus presents the results of his researches in the following work with the twofold object of saving the past of mankind from oblivion and ensuring that the extraordinary achievements of the Hellenic and Oriental worlds shall enjoy their just renown."

What was done at Thermopylae, as at Gettysburg, was an achievement. It deserved renown, and was not to pass into oblivion. "Tell them in Lakedaimon, passer-by, / That here obedient to their word we lie." If we imagine a present lacking identity with its past, and—what is the same thing—with no respect for it, we forgo all knowledge of our powers and capacities. We do not know who we are, or what we are capable of, for good or for ill, apart from what has been done. And so Ortega y Gasset says in a key sentence, "Man, in a word, has no nature; what he has is history." And again, "What nature is to things, history, *res gestae,* is to man."

Neither early man nor even Herodotus, nor any other Greek, possessed the idea of history. An "idea"—that is, a constitutional aspect of experience—doesn't come so easily and so spontaneously. It has to win its place and its authority. What actually happened in the history of thought was not the discovery of time and deeds, but of the permanent and invariable.

The idea of history waits upon the idea of nature and rises to authority only when time has been lost in the invariant, and when action has been made unintelligible by universal order. The sense of time is original, but the status of time as a constitutional factor of experience is derivative. That we are in charge of ourselves in history has not appeared plausible. It was reason, not action, wherein man first joined the universal and the free. Reason found its first alliance with the constancy through which change and variety became intelligible.

2

Motives

The actual interests that prompt men to the acts commonly regarded as historical represent more than whim and more than calculation. They are more than nature and more than intelligence.

The question, of course, is to see how that is possible. One thing seems sure, namely that if one considers a particular act, say signing the Constitution, there will always be equally particular motives. Some consideration of a very present sort will explain why action was taken at that moment. Perhaps some one of the signers had illness in the family, and wanted to hurry home. Perhaps others wanted to close a business deal, or get a drink, or get some sleep, or win a bet. The possibilities are endless. What seems important is that no remote ideal can explain why something gets done at a particular time and place. The law of gravity does not explain why the apple dropped on Newton. There are nowadays hormone sprays that keep apples from dropping. So one might argue that the law of gravity has no part in any motion. The two cases seem analogous.

The temptation comes to find history quite apart from these special impulses or calculations. But that is not satisfactory either. The ideal, when not part of the human will, never enters into action as a determiner. So there is a dilemma: What controls action seems to be impulse or calculation, and these seem to determine an act in its particularity, in its place and time; on the other side, history seems more than impulse and calculation, neither fragmentary as is impulse, nor subjectively practical like calculation. History seems more than the vagrancy of nature or the calculations that secure a personal desire. It seems rather to have style of its own, a career apart from psychology, whether chaotic or intelligent.

To explain an event historically, then, means meeting two demands: the explanation must treat the event as volitional, as part of a living purpose, and it must discover in the purpose more than the factors of accident and device. It must link an actual and particular purpose with the non-accidental, the impersonal and objective.

Let me try this again. The act and its occasion seem quite particular, and quite controlled by the particular. The universal has no consequence for the here and now. The golden rule carries no implications for pruning my apple tree in two weeks. The law of gravity does not explain or predict the fall of a leaf. There seem always to be special factors, immediate factors, at the instigation of any special change, event, or act. On the other side, it seems no less clear that the law of gravity plays some part in accounting for motion, however particular. One can't play billiards apart from gravity, any more than one can rely on gravity to drop a ball into a pocket. One chalks one's cue and keeps sober. Nor will an act occur merely on an impulse that has no authority in the character of a person, or even in the confusion of a personal character. There is, or appears to be, the steadying influence of a situation that launches the calculation or even the impulse. This steadying influence also accounts for any persistence in the calculation and gives it plausibility, or even an axiomatic propriety. One does not vote for the Constitution in order to secure trade and investments apart from the unquestioned contribution of such gains to the established ways of life. In some societies investment would not be a motive. Religion, race, power, might induce political combination, but not economics.

This is all very general and not at all conclusive. But it seems well to start with these broad suggestions. Perhaps they can be sharpened. At any rate, it seems less obvious than initially appeared plain that the particular can operate in nature or human nature without benefit of the universal. Somewhere the universal appears as an operating force in the particular.

In physics this seems well established; in human action it is less well established. This occurs because in physics the universal is no remote consequence but an ever-present law. In action, on the other hand, the universal has usually been construed as an ideal, remote, not present, and so of dubious efficacy. Only what enters into the present, the actual, and the real can operate as the determiner of the particular. The nonaccidental, the universal, must be a premise of the particular and not a remote or unrelated type of order or force.

The full story here is a long one. But in restricted terms one may say that the accidental factors always imply a universal factor. In history this universal is the environment, the circumstance, the situation, however it may be conceived, and society. To these the individual is committed, and it is this commitment that makes him an agent.

This environment is the nonpsychological or objective. Particular acts maintain it. They also serve to disclose what one takes it to be. It is the assumption that justifies the particular purpose or act.

An act maintains this environment. This is as necessary as the claim that the environment launches the act. This is the self-preservative aspect of an act. It is self-preservative because it preserves the environment with which the agent identifies himself and his values.

The more canny the act, the more "selfish" or "impure," the more it discloses the environment in terms of which it operates. Selfishness is a pathetic advertisement of one's assumed world. What selfishness does not know is that this assumed world is lawful, and hence impersonal. But selfishness is action just because it does rest in this environment. It seeks to preserve the objective through subjective device. That is its essence. That is its defect.

History is made by those who realize, however faintly,

the status of environment as the actuality of themselves. Any environment-maintaining act is historical.

Technically, an "act" that lacks the quality of maintaining its world, however vaguely, reduces to instinct. There the act and the environment merge. A cat is its world. But where there is action, the person is not only his world but the *assertion* that he is his world. This can be any world at all.

History is the maintenance of the environment. Action is the same thing. The revision of the environment is a phase of its maintenance.

This environment is always ideal. And it is always existential or actual. It is ideal because it is the orderly setting of the particular, whether fact or act. It is the immediacy of a totality. Thus it exceeds impulse and calculation. These proceed from it, and assume it.

The environment is the self in its objective mode. The self does not assert itself, know itself, or maintain itself apart from it. Self-assertion in all its forms is also environment-assertion. Thus the environment is will.

It is "pure" will. It is the will in its generic form, not particularly but universal and essential.

The bottom fallacy in the psychological interpretation of history is the assumption of act without universality—that is to say, act without commitment, without actuality and the absoluteness of the present. Wherever history is given a psychological interpretation, one will find either no environment at all, or one that is detached from the agent. He then falls back into his dreams, or else attempts to advance upon an antagonist who remains necessarily invulnerable. This is the reason for the desperation of those who would put an end to history. They know they cannot find release from an alien and indifferent antagonist. They would, therefore, deny the equation between the person and his world, and renounce objectivity because it is the occasion of will, but of a will which to them is only caprice or calculation. In this way, their initial assumption that history is always "impure" in motive leads to the skepticism of all motive, both as fact and as value. That is nihilism.

Nor can one maintain the position that history is made by men with "ulterior" motives. The purely ulterior motive would be one that regards the historical event from a point of view quite external to its own meaning or fulfillment. In the extreme—and clearest—case, this would mean an equation between the agent and some other commitment. Thus, a theocracy or its devotees might play along with democracy, using it as a steppingstone. This does not invalidate the universal factor of that action, but rather relocates it.

The ulterior motive, when purely selfish, is a myth. One needs to be downright with this point. Pure selfishness pushes ulterior motive to the vanishing point. It can live only in the moment. What makes selfishness "ulterior" also strips it of complete selfishness. What is "ulterior" in it proclaims some sort of world or environment. That is why the motive is "ulterior." A completely ulterior motive is a contradiction in terms. A motive can be asserted only at a price, and the price is some sort of objectivity. It is the objectivity with which the identity of the agent is practically assumed, but unrecognized in thought.

These considerations show that the historical is the immediate and the actual. Therein lies the impersonality of historical forces. At the same time it now appears that the particular motive is never absent, but is rather the vehicle and articulation of the universal.

3

Explanation

Cause, in general, means a ground or explaining base, a means of explaining, a condition of, the mode of understanding.

Physical causes deal only in types. A typical effect is explained by its typical antecedent or condition. That is "why" such an effect was produced. Being typical, the physical cause is not *unique*. It explains a class of events, and is itself a class of events. History, dealing with the unique, must explain the unique. Hence no typical cause will explain a historical event; only some unique cause will explain it. This unique cause will not, then, be analogous to cause in physics. It will not be the sort of cause that experiment will verify, for experiment deals in the repeatable. It will not be a cause that logic can establish, for logic requires a universal. All logical proof operates through some universal, and the conclusion justifies some attribution of a universal. But the universal is the nonhistorical.

Hence history is not to be understood as the realization of the possible. The possible is a variant of a universal. It pertains to constant conditions. Thus it is said that an earthquake is possible because of some typical geological structure. The possible requires the actual, but the actual as typical or universal. A tire may blow out if one runs over a nail; the brakes may not hold if the hydraulic system springs a leak. Unique events do not express possibility.

The idea of the possible means also that various events

might occur, and that the one occurring was not necessary, because some other event might have occurred or some other antecedent causal event might have intervened. But in physics this is not so. It is not possible in the absolute sense that brakes won't hold. They are built to hold and within the limits of control must hold. Granted the premises, it is not possible for them to slip. Physics deals in determinate possibilities and impossibilities, not absolute possibilities or impossibilities. Within limits, physics is not guesswork. Some other event could not have occurred within these limits.

But the unique historical event is not viewed as having a determinate possibility or impossibility. Being unique, it occurs in an infinite context. Brutus might have come down with appendicitis and so never have reached the Forum on the ides of March. He might have tripped and suffered a concussion going up the steps of the senate. Here the possible is something formless and indeterminate. One could never say just what other event was possible. One could never prove it. One could only mean that in the unique, one has an infinite context.

The past does not explain the present in physics. *Post hoc, ergo propter hoc* is invalid in physics. Yet in history the past is somehow needed to explain, to understand the present.

The past cannot illuminate a present that is to be understood only in terms of uniform law. But the past is certainly not irrelevant in matters of growth—for example, in psychiatry. A peculiar sort of control is invoked when the past is allowed to be efficacious. The past is the definition of the order of growth. This holds for both psychology and dialectic. To deny all efficacy to the past is to deny all growth, all change capable of defining time.

Change in physics does not define time, a past. What exists in physics is the invariant. That is the only item neither needing explanation nor capable of explanation. What should be or may be explained does not define any mode of discourse. Physics needs to explain any event that is different from any other. Its being different shows that it is not fundamental but derived.

In history, all difference is original, not to be seen in terms other than itself. Originality is ontological. In physics, difference is not ontological. It is derivative.

Originality is the differences that make a world in which there is action. Absence of originality implies absence of act. Absence of act implies absence of originality.

An original difference requires some sort of order other than that of the natural science with its uniformities, none of which is original.

Science explains what is *not* original.

History explains what is original.

The original differences, like the exemplary differences, need to be understood.

Original differences can be understood only in the disequilibrium of some point of view.

Physics invokes the ideally complete; history, the ideally incomplete.

Physics changes in the direction of unification; history, in the direction of diversity and variety. In history, we must be sure not to read the events of one place and one time as if their place and their time were irrelevant. What is done is always of its own place and time. Novels, dress, views of nature and the supernatural, education, and sex are to be seen in their specific occasions alone.

In history, the past is a cause because the past is a factor in understanding the present.

But the past, although a cause, is not to be known without the result. The past is not to be separated from the effect. In nature, whether any event is to be the cause of another depends on circumstance. The cause can be isolated. It can appear without the effect. If a natural cause could not be known as an event without the effect, its causal relation to the effect could not be discovered. The cause is known by our ability to prevent its operation.

It is this feature of cause that is essential to its discovery and meaning. It is not the case that the causal order is there, and that then we derange it. The causal order is not there until we do derange it.

Nature, we may think, goes its way, our desires to the contrary notwithstanding. It is true that our desires do not change nature. Wishes leave its ways untouched. But what those ways are, while not affected by our wishes, is unknown apart from our action. I may or may not wish to have rain; but seeding clouds is a way of getting rain.

The facts do not reflect our wishes; they do reflect our acts. To find out nature's ways is no wish. Everyone knows that what we then find out is the ways of a region quite aloof to wishes.

Nature is not controlled as a secondary reaction; it is defined through control.

No control implies no nature in any intelligible sense.

The nature that goes its own way is not so alien and fierce as one might suppose. One never quite means the harshness or indifference of nature to be absolute. Nature could not be so independent until it was defined, and before that it was the gods who were our masters.

Nature is an absolute order known only because of our own action which, in preventing an event, lays bare its cause.

4

Cause

History, as a mode of order, has no cause. No mode of order has a cause. Thus mathematics and logic have no causes. But any event *within* any mode of order has a cause. This is the same as saying that there is a way of understanding that event, that it is not an unrelated catastrophe. Cause is the reason that places an event within some order. Each mode of order has its own mode of reason. The cause of the equivalence of the internal angles of a triangle to two right angles is of a different form from the cause of yellow fever or the cause of the motion of the tides. In all cases one cites the reason for the event, or fact, or situation. Aristotle's four "causes" illustrate this basic identity of cause with the mode of understanding or accounting for an event. The rejection of final causes means only that such controls have no force or explanatory power in nature. The reason of nature is then alleged not to involve final causes.

An event in history has a cause in the sense that it falls within the order of history and is not, therefore, an independent event or catastrophe. The adoption of the Constitution is, let us suppose, a historical event. We may and, indeed, must ask its causes—that is, the system of reason that controls it. This event, let us assume, is not in nature but in human nature. It will not have the sort of rationale proper to the tides or to a fire in the wastebasket. It is an event incomprehensible at any other time or place. It is unique. It is not a typical event, like the tides or the fire. But, though unique, it is not a catastrophe, unrelated to other events of its own peculiar sort. It occurred in a context, a human context, but nevertheless one related to other events. In that relation lies its cause. This relation involves its antecedents. The antecedents are the American mind. It was this temper that adopted the Constitution and revealed itself in that act.* This antecedent temper is a cause in the sense that it saves the adoption from being a catastrophe, without order, reason, or linkage with other events. This temper had shown itself in other events prior to the adoption. It was itself peculiar, not easily identified or understood, but neither was it unknown. It too had had a career. The union of the colonies seems not to have been an inscrutable surprise to anyone. It had been preceded by the Confederation, and by a war involving a degree of co-operation. There had, also, been much talk of union even before the war.

It is true that one could not antecedently know that the union would occur. But this is not to say that it had no antecedents. It is only to say that the antecedents of a historical event are never known apart from their consequences. Where there is will, there is always obscurity as to its implications. What will take place in the career of will is always a function of circumstance. It is always improvised for the occasion. And the circumstances themselves have a changing meaning to the will as it unfolds and becomes clearer to itself. A will cannot, indeed, find its own clarity apart from the circumstances in the face of which it is maintained. A more perfect union came to be seen as a consequence of the earlier will to independence. Only so could the fruits of independence be fully matured and enjoyed.

In this way, the will in its career has an essential element of passivity. The will, as absolute action, is also absolute

---

*The unidentifiability of cause apart from effect is not peculiar to history. No event, as causal, is unqualified by its effects. The irrelevance of effect to cause would leave no way of discovering the cause, no way of selecting it.

passivity. To will is to accept the consequences of self-definition. But these consequences are always asserted in the context of circumstance, of which the bearing on the will is always itself a revelation. It is this will that identifies circumstances and gives them systematic importance. The cause of a historical event is therefore (1) the actual existence of a will and (2) its continued assertion, or maintenance, in the face of circumstance. Such is the order, or rationale, of history.

Causes are identified in so far as control occurs. This holds for *all* causes, for all reasons, and for all understanding. But history is control in principle. It is the maintenance of control. There is no cause of control, no control of control, no reason for it, and no understanding of it. But this does not imply that a particular case of such pure control has no cause or reason. On the contrary, every case of pure control demands a clear perception of the confusion that it seeks to avoid, and recognizes the actual circumstances that threaten control. The cause of a historical event can, then, be identified in a threat, but not in a fact. The threat is, of course, occasioned by the facts, but by the facts in their relevance to an existent will. History is articulated in the threats of annihilation that circumstance offers to a will.

This is the concreteness of history, its perpetual tentativeness and unpredictability in detail. The modes of control are various, but all modes are productive of history. Apart from its engagement with circumstance, the will is abstract and ceases to be actual—that is, active. History need not fear the contributory factor of circumstance as a rational ingredient. One need only be clear on the manner of that contribution. The will defines its own circumstances, but does not abolish them. An abstract cause, such as a glowing cigarette, does not define its actual circumstances.

The circumstances that history defines and exploits are various. They include nature and human purposes. Both nature and psychology are causes of history in the standard sense of being factors in making history intelligible.

Nature and psychology are defined through will, not as antagonists, but as the materials exploited by will. They are no more antagonists of will than ink is an antagonist of notemakers. Nature and psychology conspire to permit will to attain specific form. While the absence of plague or earthquake does not explain the specific event called the adoption of the Constitution, yet physiological and geologic factors operate in permitting the historical event to occur. Nature always carries in its pocket a veto for any human act. When one says, then, that a natural condition is a factor in historical events, one means that history is impossible apart from the silent support of nature.

Analogously, a historical event includes in its rationale psychological factors of a permissive sort. The desire for good business or for the payment of the debts incurred by the colonies during the war induces some, or may have induced some, to vote for adoption of the Constitution. Such psychological attitudes are, then, factors in explaining the actual adoption in a particular place and time. They do not explain what made the adoption historical, but they do help to explain how the historical event actually occurred.

Furthermore, such contributing factors as nature and psychology are not, in principle, accidental. No historical process is possible without them. The career of the will is for most persons obscure. And in the measure that the will is complex, and the modes of its actuality are various, support for the acts that are history-making cannot be equally disinterested for all who participate. The narrow intensity required of the maker of history will be peculiar to his own mind, or to few minds. Others can be brought to co-operate, but for reasons not clearly and deliberately demanding the historical act. Some phases of will must be unrecognized by some persons who nevertheless support that will. Some persons, for example, "enjoy" music, but do not feel the compulsions that produced it. They will support an orchestra for all sorts of reasons, including the most trivial. This situation is a necessary one. The musician in turn may see political freedom as desirable only because it allows music to be sold to a large public. He will support a school that teaches physics while, perhaps, having no feeling for the historical meaning of physics. In general, for most people, most historical events have no historical force, yet without their consent and co-operation those events would not take place.

Thus nature and psychology conspire to allow history to be made. The very man who makes history will have but a vague understanding of all the instrumentalities that he employs. He will use language, or logic, or physics, or religion in order to carry his point. Reason in history includes the accidents of nature and the irresponsibilities of psychology. This inclusion is necessary. History-making is perilous. The history-maker must act now. He must be ready to act with the aid of nature and psychology. He cannot wait until all minds have joined his.

5

Purpose

History deals with acts. Hence, with purpose. But it deals with purpose as the process that revises it, not as the process that executes it.

For example, I wish to play tennis. Hence I wear flat-soled shoes. Wearing the shoes executes the purpose, or part of it. It is a means to an end already accepted. I wish to win a battle, to get new territory; I build an army, secure equipment, and learn strategy. Here again there is a specific purpose and specific means to carry it out. All that is conscious, deliberate, intellectual. The only success is a success of means, the only failure, one of means. Success and failure are thus technical. There is no way of judging the value of playing tennis, or of winning a war. One simply begins by declaring tennis or war.

In so far as the tennis and the war reflect no larger environment to which they are adjustments and expressions, they are not values, and hence cannot be said to be purposes. They cannot be said to be *acts*. No *person* is merely a tennis player or a soldier. A person plays tennis in the interests of a more inclusive program. Were this not so, one would be back to mechanism or to catastrophe. There would then be tennis and war, but not anybody engaging in them. They would either just happen, or else be part of a causal sequence. But that is not purpose, not act, not history.

For a person to play tennis, the game is no absolute. It suits one's situation. It is played because it suits. Nothing that suits is wholly conscious. One commits oneself to *some* course of action—as one must in order to act at all—and specific acts then become suitable. Thus, in college one has no debate over athletic exercise, assuming good health. Nor does one make a study of all sports and select tennis. Tennis is a local sport, one lives here, so one plays tennis. Every specific act emerges from a matrix of commitment, a commitment necessary in principle, but accidental in its content. In England one plays cricket; in the United States, baseball. The possibility of a specific act involves the necessity of a program already under way. That program is something that just happens to one. That there is *some* program is no accident.

If tennis is no absolute, but dependent upon its suitability, the particular view of things that leads to tennis—say, going to college—is also no absolute. The same considerations apply to all specific elements in motive or action; they are both necessary in principle and accidental in their peculiarity.

For that reason they are all unstable. Their contingency (or accidental aspect) bespeaks their restless demand for enlargement. To become conscious of the accidental is to see its limits; and to see limits is to apprehend the next factor, the environment of a limit. So one sees that one goes to college because of the times and the place, but one sees that there are other times and places, and thus going to college becomes one's conscious will, or else wins rejection as something unsuitable.

The essence of a purposive act is not only that it proceeds from a general program but also that it requires the revision of the program in the interests of which it is undertaken.

To go merely forward is either causality or chaos, and to go merely backward is to inhibit all action. Thus also in logic: to move downward from premises prohibits the assertion of fact, premises being hypothetical; and to move ever backward is equally frustrating. Hence there is an inherently irrational factor in action (and in thought), namely in the fact of action (and thought) itself.

Whether one deals with the acts of individuals or of groups, this revision of the basis of action is necessary, for it defines action. Without it, there is no purpose. But what governs this revision? Merely the necessity of will, its search for itself, for its clarity in detail, and for its own being as will. History *is* will. It is the career of will. History is the progressive clarification of will. It has no ulterior goal. Confusion results from supposing that history tends to a specific end. Rather, it exists for its own sake, for the sake of maintaining itself as action. Thus its search is for freedom, for freedom is the self-maintaining activity of will.

The cessation of history is the dogmatic, the refusal to revise specific conditions of acts. Hence revolution is peculiarly historical.

Events in time play a role in history only as they involve a revision of the premises of action. Events are historical only as they affect values and thus lead to new types of action. Without that revision of values no act has been performed, for the mark of act is will, and the mark of will is freedom, and the mark of freedom is self-revision.

Hence the turbulence of history, both personal and social. For there can be no conscious will apart from impulse and the consequent discovery of the extent to which it represents limitation.

Thus the necessity of the nonrational establishes the superiority of direction. For direction can be discovered only through the impulsive and without the direction the impulsive is no longer defective. Without the direction it could not be defined as impulse, for each impulse would then be absolute, hence neither rational nor opposed to the rational, but an independent world.

If one plays tennis one finds out the place of tennis, and only by playing it can one discover the values of the way of life that suggests tennis. It may not be tennis, but it must be *some* act. This is merely to say that to correct values one must begin by asserting *some* value, and hence must act. But the value asserted, being accidental, discloses its partiality only in the partial failure of the acts that it provokes. The limitation of a point of view, of a set of values, of an outlook, could get no other disclosure. *To act at all is to confess limits,* for omnipotence need not act, and cannot act. Only limitation needs to preserve itself in action. (Hence the passions of acts, due to their blindness and to their insistency.) One must be more than a tennis player to play tennis. Consequently the partiality of the satisfaction of tennis challenges the attitude that requires one to play it. One gets tired, one can't work, or one succeeds and neglects other things—say, studies. Or, one may see only good in it, and thus become more aware of the place of the way of life that includes tennis.

In sum, history is action, and action is will, and will is both purpose and the revision of purpose, and the revision of purpose is freedom, having no end other than the maintenance of action itself. Act is limitation, and hence exploration. The form of exploration is the philosophy of history. For no one can assert history as action apart from the order of action; there is no difference between action and its implicit order. Action is the order of the will. To deny the order is to abolish the possibility of finding either the act or the will.

Hence history can be told only in terms of what men learn. But what they learn is history only as they learn about *the conditions of action*—that is, of freedom. To learn that a lob pulls a player back in the court is not history; to learn that square-rigged ships go fastest is not history. But Newton and Einstein make history because they change the meaning of the facts. Thus history is the story not of intellect, but of the relation of intellect to programs of action.

Most history teaching is in the worst sense "academic." It is not the story of how men learn to revise premises. It is not the career of *destiny,* but only a psychologically entertaining adventure. No history can be taught as such apart from a conception of how one can learn, and must learn. If one can't learn and if learning has no direction, then there is no history. All that history can teach at last is that there *is* history. This basic proposition can then be illustrated from the so-called facts. That is all the facts are good for. But that is what they *are,* and that is how they happen to be facts, acts, deeds, things done.

6

*Psychology**

History involves the question, How can one understand the causes of this act or this event? If one answers that all acts are to be understood only psychologically, then there is no history at all, but only psychology. One must answer that some acts have nonpsychological causes.

Obviously, the question of rationale must assume the character of the act or event to be explained. What one takes the act to be is what will control the explanation. Consequently an assumption of an act with nonpsychological causes postulates an act that is, by definition, a free act. Without that assumption, or some such assumption, one could argue that there are no acts at all, since all alleged acts are then only physical change. In so far as an act is viewed in the rationale of physics or psychology, it is not in the discourse of history at all.

The question, How can an act with none but psychological explanations be part of history? can only be answered by saying that it cannot possibly be part of history. If the Constitution was, or possibly was, adopted *only* for psychological reasons, it is no part of history.

Where, then, to find history?

(1) Perhaps there are acts quite without psychology. For many reasons, this seems to me impossible.

(2) Perhaps all acts with psychology have a disinterested

*See also John William Miller, "History and Case History," *The American Scholar,* Spring 1980, pp. 241–43.—ED.

ingredient. This I affirm, in so far as psychology is interpreted as self-seeking.

(3) Perhaps some acts have nonpsychological causes in the motives of some men, and psychological causes in the motives of others. That is to say, the nonpsychological factor may become the explicit factor for some, while only the implicit factor for others. This I affirm.

(4) Perhaps in some acts the nonpsychological factor occurs for some men as a matter of abstract principle, for others as a matter of genuine historical feeling, and both of these accompany ordinary psychological motives for a third group. This I affirm.

(5) But I affirm further that none of these acts is properly historical until it has been reflected upon after it has been done. History needs the historian. Not until a later act is directed toward disinterestedness by an earlier one is the earlier act part of history. But this permits the psychological act to enter history in so far as the historian discovers the nonpsychological conditions of the psychological act. This seems to me a very important part of history. It is enormously useful in disclosing the organizations of will apropos of which the psychological occurs. The absolute must first appear in its unrecognized particular interpretations. It cannot be original.

Very few history-making acts meet the conditions of being neither psychological nor abstractly absolute. Yet history has been made; the secular has been the sacred. That is impossible apart from either the immanence of history, which I affirm, or its transcendence, which I deny. So it comes to the immanence of history.

For that immanence the historian searches. It is the real cause, the final cause. But he finds it not as fact, but as the control of his identification of the facts. This, in turn, is the meaning of his own reflections. The historical event is any event that allows historical reflection. I affirm that all psychological acts offer that opportunity.

It is for that reason that the act of John Hancock, who supported the Constitution in the hope of becoming president, enters into history. One can reflect on its meaning.

Merely the fact that that act aided in the formation of the Constitution does not make it historical. So far it is as accidental as the weather or the good health of the signers. On the other hand, maybe all the signers were no better motivated. Then all one can say of their act is that the later consideration of its motives discloses the value put upon a chance to hold office or to do business, that for these things men will run great risks, that these things must be affirmed as absolutely valuable.

7

Accidents

Specific events in history are frequently explained through a specific accident. For example, the victory of Gates over Burgoyne may have been due to the failure of Howe to move up from New York, and Howe's absence may be explained by the failure of Lord Germain to dispatch to Howe an order to join Burgoyne. Thus the very important surrender at Saratoga, perhaps a decisive event in the American Revolution, may be traced to Lord Germain's oversight.

Perhaps a clearer case of the influence of accident is the capture of Lee's battle plan prior to the action at Antietam.

The characteristic form of the influence of an accident consists of a purpose that is aided or defeated by the occurrence of an event outside the calculations made for carrying out that purpose. Any purpose requires a minimum of control, a minimal area from which accident is excluded. In the illustration offered above, McClellan and Lee had enough control to permit the movement and engagement of troops. This meant that there were available men, organization, food, transport, and ammunition. Some parts of the environment were under control. No control at all means no plan at all. All action presumes a minimal control of objects, some identification of object and will. A plan without control is a fantasy.

Only where some purpose and its attendant control are assumed can an accident be influential. Only there can it operate. Accidents deflect a purpose from its goal, or make the goal possible, where the calculated purpose, apart from the accident, would have succeeded or failed. Every purpose makes enormous assumptions. Every purpose recognizes the region of ignorance and so of the incalculable. But most purposes succeed without benefit of specific accident because they operate within the limits of an environment that is part of the purpose itself. For example, one could fail to carry out one's purpose to go to the post office because a storm had felled a tree and the tree had carried down dangerous electric wires, blocking the street. But one's purpose to go to the post office falls within a habitual environment. One's residence was chosen because of its proximity to the post office, because of one's ability to walk there, because of the normal accessibility of the post office. Most purposes are of this sort. They operate within the environment which they have created, and which in turn sustains them. This created environment is full of accidents, but the environment itself, and the purposes which sustain it, are not at the hazard of accidents. The storm may fell a tree, but the debris will be cleared away. Or one can post one's letter by going a roundabout way.

Ordinary purposes do not, therefore, make us aware of the influence of accidents. We remain within the habitual. Our habits are disturbed by accidents, but such disturbances do not derange the stability of broad purposes. Those purposes go on. They continue. Accidents in the habitual region are inconvenient, but decisive neither for radical failure nor for radical success. Radical success is in the existence of that environment; radical failure, only in its disappearance.

Where an accident is supposed to determine history, it is the sort of event that decides what the habitual environment is to be. That is why accidents within the environment seem relatively unimportant. They are taken for granted, along with the environment and its purposes. Our dealing with such accidents may even lead to the belief that the environment is subject to, or under comfortable control of, purposes.

The historically decisive accident is peculiar to the historically decisive purpose. Historical purposes, like all others, are subject to the influence of the accidental. Indeed, it is only where purpose takes on the full dimensions of history-making will that the accident looms as a fateful factor. Only there, in its relation to a self-defining purpose, can the accidental appear as a factor of universal and inescapable influence. The decisive power of the accident is complementary to the finality of the will that it can further or cancel. The historical will is the marginal will. It occurs only where the risk is itself fateful. It represents the minimum for which one will accept settlement. In complement to it, the accident anounces the hazard of the will as it seeks to make itself concrete and actual. Yet the accident that touches the historical will emerges from the same region of nature that the will has already appropriated. The accident is not arbitrary.

Where the accident can be arbitrary, no historical will is possible, for then action is itself magic, in a world of equally incalculable magic. The historical will must wait upon a view of nature that identifies nature with the actuality of will.★ Where nature is alien to will no history is possible, and no accident can suggest either a broad rightness of one's plans or their detailed inadequacy. Accidents occur to purpose from the same region in which the purpose finds its actuality. For that reason every historical commitment is the assertion of the region that makes history possible, namely nature in all its lawful identity with the will itself.

But nature in this intimate association with the historical will extends to the same infinity as one's own endeavors. Consequently it is also infinitely unexplored, and always threatens to intrude into the small plans made, to establish its own laws, and to give them an actual power as the form of action itself.

★When nature is not itself an ingredient in will and personality, no reason can be given for not treating it as more than a fashionable eccentricity that one may relinquish at any time. As with an impulse to take exercise, one can always lie down until it has passed.

History thus defines nature. Nature is both the cause and the limit of every unconditioned resolve. Without history, nature remains a phantom, an appearance only, arbitrary and incoherent, a set of thoughts, without capacity to resist the will because not defined through the will. On the other side, the will vanishes when nature is given a merely intellectual or phenomenal status.

The accident is the hazard that the will encounters in being actual.

The occurrence of accidents does not show that history is at the mercy of nature. Nature, as surely, is at the mercy of history. Nature has no power over will except the power that it secures by being part of the will itself. Action defines the infinity that in specific occasions can nullify purposes. The cure for the failure of such purposes is further knowledge of nature. In that knowledge, called natural science, the success of purposes becomes more assured. But to know nature is not to find external means for purposes irrelevant to nature. The knowledge of nature is itself history-making and in principle makes history possible. To ignore nature is to leave purposes arbitrary.

Nevertheless, every marginal will must be forever subject to extinction by the intrustion of nature, that nature which it invokes and affirms but can never wholly encompass. It cannot encompass nature, because nature is only its own infinity, not an alien infinity that would be without power to affect finite actuality.

In the main, those who stand with nature will succeed. They will maximally reduce the risk that besets the marginal will. Such a will best respects itself.

8

*The Static Ideal**

There has always been a great temptation to reduce history to something else. It has lacked the flavor of a quite original and independent mode of construing experience and reality. It fell, perhaps, within the supernatural and its controls were not in itself. Sometimes, it became a species of physics, man being regarded as an inconsiderable piece of matter, and under the sway of those laws and forces that moved the stars or arranged the atoms. There are those who see it as psychology, as social or even as abnormal psychology. Indeed, what with the supernatural, the physical order, and the psychological world of appearance and blind impulse, history has lurked in the shadows of scientific respectability.

In addition to these formidable intellectual authorities, history has had to make head against ethics, or what has passed for ethics and morality. For the man concerned to do right, to carry out his duties and attain perfection of will, human conduct has seemed better guided by the Ten Commandments than by a knowledge of past acts. Leaving aside theology, the answer to what man is, it has seemed, should be sought in science; the answer to what

*See also "The Ahistoric and the Historic," Afterword by John William Miller to José Ortega y Gasset, *History as a System* (New York: W. W. Norton & Company, 1961), pp. 237–69; and John William Miller, "The Ahistoric Ideal," in *The Paradox of Cause* (New York: W. W. Norton & Company, 1978), pp. 130–60.—Ed.

man ought to do, in ethics. Between these two—the truth about man and the duty of man—we have, on the whole, felt that all useful knowledge was shared. There are the facts or the truth, and there is our duty and our salvation. What more does one want, or could one want?

The principal vehicles of acceptable knowledge in our time are mathematics and the natural sciences, particularly physics and chemistry. Although entirely humanistic and secular in origin and development, they have perpetuated the static ideal. Their content has no dates. It is true that physics includes time, but it is a repeatable time, as in the formula for gravitational motion, $S = \frac{1}{2}gt^2$. All bodies move freely in accordance with that rule, at all calendar dates, and at all places. It is the repeatable quality of events in nature that permits experiment. Experiments cannot be made on the unique, but only on the uniform. It is this uniformity under many particular guises that is searched out by the experimenter. The common world is thereby established. In contrast with its impersonal majesty our personal lives may well appear trivial and chaotic.

Yet it took time for the sciences to grow and they are still in process of transformation and enlargement. Pythagoras and Euclid and their successors have defined space. There is no natural object called space which can be seen with the eye or upon which one can perform some act, as one can eat meat or throw a stone. To make space an object at all is the same as studying geometry and physics. Space is, as we say, an object of thought alone, not of sense. There is no sense organ for its perception. It has no meaning from the practical point of view of solving any particular problem. Mathematics and physics are not consequences of any particular physiological organ or of an act resulting from the adaptation of that organ to another specific situation. One can take hold of objects because of the construction of the hand and especially of the opposable thumb. But the statements of mathematics and physics fall back on no such particular organ, object, or act. These sciences do not sketch the observable properties of nature, however general or widespread those properties may be. Rather, they present the very region of nature.

The order of nature, the continuum of quantity, space, and motion, has meaning only in these sciences, and one must study them in order to have nature before one as a region. In the case of mathematics especially, the immensity of the order there revealed has often struck the poetic and religious imagination. Without these sciences, nature as a region has no meaning and all action reduces to impulse and to the opportunism of the moment. Action without regard to the over-all constitution of nature can satisfy no need but appetite. The ancient scientists were well aware of this, and they looked to the study of these sciences as the living alternative to the dark slavery of disorderly impulses. Plato felt that the study of mathematics furnished a discipline for vagrancy. It did this because its concern lay in the nonaccidental, in the necessary and universal. Science furnishes an outlook; appetite can only seize the moment, and then fall away into the lethargy of satiety.

Yet these vast, and even immense, adventures of thought have no warrant beyond their human appeal. They are the actuality of thought. They are the loci of systematic control. In science, thought is all our own, but it is not vagrant. There it encounters discipline and self-definition. Nature and thought display identical laws. Those who can see man only as appetite do not take kindly to any story of secular disinterestedness. But science in all its forms is the wholly disinterested definition of nature as a region. For those who have dwelt in this discipline of thought the traditional restraints on appetite seem hardly less gross than the appetites themselves. Common crimes go against nature because they are the means of losing one's grasp on the moods and attitudes that lead to nature as an order and as a region. Euclid is a better moral guide than Moses.

Nature is the discipline of the secular and of the finite. It is more than a catalogue of subjective impressions. It is rational because it is infinite and therefore no object of perception or of sense. It is the order of experience in principle. It is pure act and pure thought. It is the actuality of our powers working in time, with constant revision and even revolutions. As experience, nature is not a *fait accompli,* but the ever-modified organization of the objective in principle.

For these reasons there is no science without history. History is the process by which sciences become established, distinguished, and modified. But for all that, the content of science is the static, not the process by which views of the static become transformed. Nature comes to stand for the ahistoric and is commonly so viewed. It is usually regarded as being, in ideal, a closed system within which change is only an episode, an illustration of timeless laws. The weight of this very general belief upon the authenticity of history has been enormous. Historians have been put in the position of dealing only with appearances of nature while the scientists deal with nature directly as the source and cause of the phenomena upon which the historian makes his report.

This tendency has had a wider scope than the subsumption of history to physics. It has swept into its current all the humanities. Psychology has become a study of phenomena or of objects treated as having their primary definition through the region of centimeters, grams, seconds, and volts. To assert the independence of any distinctively psychological concept has come to be regarded as convincing evidence of superstition. At the most, there is a shadowy entity called the "organism" which is to adjust itself to its "environment." This organism, it seems, can "learn." But strenuous efforts are made to avoid the implications of these terms. It is all to be viewed as reflex and physiology, and so, in the end, there is no adjustment at all, but the prolongation of nature into every "response" or act. The reflex has been much employed as the link of psychology with physics—an act of pure desperation, since there are no reflexes in physics. It would be profitable to get the pot to boil without using gas as one blew a whistle or uttered a magic hocus-pocus. These possibilities are intriguing. But it is all great nonsense, which has nevertheless occupied serious thinkers. And here too one is

regarded with incredulity or with patronage when one asks
about the possible autonomy of psychology, where perception and memory, learning and act, are to be regarded
as of no less original status in defining nature than the
yardsticks, causes, and equations of physics.

When we went to school we studied "government."
Now our children take courses in "political science." This
new term gives the proper note of alliance with the natural
sciences. Anthropology is having a great vogue because
here it is hoped and believed man and society can best be
studied as phenomena and the various patterns of culture
set out as events that happen in nature. In one way or
another human nature has come to be regarded in many
quarters as a fact to be observed and reported on, if possible and ideally, in the terms of statistics and physics. In all
three cases the ideal of knowledge is the ahistoric. It is
assumed that truth is not in the telling and knowledge not
in the knowing. The very interesting and altogether plausible result of this attitude is the reduction of language to
a phenomenon of nature. This tendency should be given
welcome, since it is the inevitable outcome of the ideal of
knowledge that repudiates time. All languages are dead, if,
indeed, one may assume a distinction between the living
and the dead without begging the question. But, certainly,
on the assumption that knowledge aims at the disclosure
of a universal order, and that all change can be understood
only in terms of such order, it follows that language can be
understood only in terms of nature, and never nature in
terms of language.

Truth and knowledge thus become allied with the static,
with a region of inexorable and universal uniformity of
which all change is only the vehicle and embodiment. This
tendency has received notable help from the Baconian idea
that "knowledge is power" and that "nature, to be com-
manded, must be obeyed." This claim, made in the interests of emancipation from dogma and sterile logic, has
taken strong hold. But it has become transformed into the
cult of administration and management. Men can be managed as well as nature, since men are only part of nature's

impersonal order. Here again one sees a profoundly ahistoric tendency, the aversion of thought to time and its
preoccupation with the static. The management of men
now becomes not only possible but desirable. Whoever
denies this is held guilty of "rationalization," the substitu-
tion of "good" reasons for "real" reasons. Any claim to
originality of control is reduced to psychology, very likely
to abnormal psychology, since the failure to see the real as
factual nature is an infallible sign of wishful thinking. Consequently art becomes the evidence of a mind that has
failed and now takes out its failures in dreams and protes-
tations. Religion, of course, has been thoroughly psy-
choanalyzed, as have ethics and every other venture into
the law as self-control.

The supernatural is likewise ahistoric, fixed and immutable and usually cherished partly for that very reason. It is
the unmoved mover, the first cause itself uncaused, the
complete and perfect, without error, defect, or aspiration.
It is the self-contained, containing all else, unchallenged,
invulnerable. Its plans are not translatable into our values
nor our values into its timeless sufficiency. Indeed, the
more one considers the penchant of men for keeping a
record of the past, the more remarkable this interest
appears. Knowledge, it may well appear, is either in nature
study or else in the supernatural revelation. To make, or
hope to make, an object of knowledge out of the acts of
men when action is so plainly the advertisement of limit
seems preposterous. Consequently it is not to be wondered
at that history has often been viewed as disclosing some
nonhistorical background of which history is an episode.

In our time this background is nature. For Saint Augustine it was the plan of God. For Marxists it is the curious
objective process called the dialectic of matter. Others have
seen history as moral or intellectual progress. But in all
these cases one can note the need of treating history as finding its value in some ahistoric reality, natural or supernatural, moral, intellectual, or merely psychological. And
what needs remembering is that this demand reflects no
arbitrary prejudice, but the reasonable and plausible out-

9

Mistrust of Time

Suspicion of time is a special instance of a general uneasiness over all the modes of ordered finitude. Reason itself leaves our most responsible moments contingent upon consequences that come to no final termination and upon premises that, if they are not arbitrary or miraculous, call for an ever more remote support. Nor is a man's virtue unalterably established, but must prove itself again in new circumstances for which an earlier composure may be inadequate. Let a man look at any of the modes of his articulate functioning and he will find that not one has escaped the charge of futility. The fortress of order has become vulnerable in the degree that its architecture and construction have been most impervious to episodic assault. Every castle is a Castle Perilous, for it is designed as a guard against an environing situation that reasserts its presence and its power in the very stones that can fend off the casual invader. There is no basis for a mistrust of time until action and thought have taken shape and style. It is in the structured temple of delight, not in formless abandon, that veiled Melancholy has her sovereign shrine.

There has been, indeed, many a way to arrest time, and art, not least, draws us from our anxieties: "Thou, silent form, dost tease us out of thought / As doth eternity." The lover, the thinker, the poet, the hedonist, are in agreement with the ascetic. None trusts to time, and each looks for a present intensity that endows the moment with intrinsic worth. These absorptions often appear to mark a soft life, and are looked upon with suspicion by earnest persons who see them as truants from the work of the world. But there is a lust of battle, too, where great resolve can lift men to their finest hour. "Now, God be thanked, Who has matched us with His hour, / And caught our youth, and wakened us from sleeping." Some seize upon the day, others are seized by the emergencies of thought or of action, but all rejoice in an absorption that asks no question about tomorrow. Even sober thinkers place some emphasis on present exertion.

Sometimes the immediate exerts its force not as an argued release but as passion and splendor. The safety of habit may be disrupted by some demanding abandonment. "She has heard a whisper say, / A curse is on her if she stay / To look down to Camelot." But, then, within a bowshot from her bower eaves there passed Sir Lancelot: "She left the web, she left the loom," and found disaster. " 'The curse has come upon me!' cried / The Lady of Shalott." Time has no delusions unless one invites them, but not to make this venture is to forgo not only desire but every declaration of an instant integrity, every quickening concentration of selfhood. A poised and aloof contemplation that sees the passions and hungers of men as a victimization must face the counterclaim of wholeness in the summary and shining moment, whether pleasant or passionate. We cannot very well be "up and doing, / With a heart for any fate" without some occasion that summons the will to its uttermost and thereby takes chances with a cosmic totality that, like the placid mirror, is shattered by the passage of Sir Lancelot.

Sometimes we have tried to elude time and fortune for the sake of a momentary adequacy. Even our ideals, unless they are empty, have enforced the importance of their temporal vehicles. And sometimes a rush of rapture brings a commanding intensity to a present and rescues us from a pale nonentity. And yet these enlivening moments betray themselves to their environments. Time and circumstance reassert their presence and, in the measure that we have disqualified them, spoil a finality that has borrowed its meaning from a personal past or from an evasiveness that haunts and shadows its pretended sufficiency. Horace could not count on a pleasant dinner with his friends if he had not seen to it that olives and grapes had been planted and pruned. Besides, he liked his Falernian to be well aged. One may prefer cash and wish to let the credit go, but sometimes it is a convenience to draw on one's credit, particularly if one has a desire for cakes and ale. Good credit, like good wine, is not available in the present tense. In the end it is the hedonist who is solidly seduced by virtuous regularity of conduct. The difficulty with hedonism is not that it is possible but (alas!) naughty; it is rather that even the high moment requires some environment, if only the crude circumstance of facts. And facts relevant to the supply of desire must themselves be supplied by thought and forethought.

Nor did the mystic find the occasion of flights into ecstasy until mindless savagery had been supplanted by institutional refinements, and the abrupt discontinuity of uncontrolled reactions had taken on the decorum of form, as if the intimations of eternity had to be provided by a prior grace in speech and custom. The "pure nothingness" of Meister Eckhart depends on a legacy of doctrine that included the idea that the word had become flesh and dwelt among us. Nothingness does not generate the mystical flight. "When me they fly, I am the wings" applies to the manifold, quite as much as to Brahma, although the writer of the *Upanishad* seems not to have thought so, and Emerson himself never quite came to terms with death and taxes.

It seems, indeed, not possible to view time as a region that one may enter should one wish to do so, or avoid if that appears the advantageous course. If time stood as an object of intelligent choice, all these emotional essays of accommodation would be much overdone. My friend who lives in Vermont finds the winters there pretty rugged, but he knows quite well that he could move to Massachusetts, where twenty-five below zero Fahrenheit is more rare, or to Florida, where it is unknown. There are some particulars that one cannot usually evade, such as one's height or complexion, but these do not arouse the interest and eloquence of poets, philosophers, and theologians. When such particulars constrain attention they stifle rather than enlarge the imagination and restrict feeling to an obsessive narrowness.

Our relations with time are total and constitutive. The emotions and theories that have been provoked when time has seemed unsatisfactory permeate the whole man and affect his entire outlook. Remedies for the ills of time are not analogous to those appropriate to particular uneasiness. Limited ills respond to specific remedies, but limitation itself, as an over-all condition, can hardly be amended by some patent medicine or by a change in diet. We can with some plausibility abandon our purposes, declaring all of them unprofitable, but what we cannot do is appraise the whole region of purpose from a point of view which itself expresses any finite purpose. Where one has a constitutional problem no "theory of types," no more inclusive tentativeness, is of the slightest use. And so we have tried to arrest a fickle fortune in oblivious pleasure or by reaching for a steady "reality" where, in the absence of a perilous present, there are to be no yesterdays and no tomorrows.

Such desperate remedies indicate a vague and troubled uncertainty over the identity of the actual person, not a reasonable choice among more or less advantageous alternatives. Choice, deliberate and informed, has its place; but it is not, as many have said, the avenue leading to emancipation. It is a dubious therapy that can only perpetuate the conditions of distress. The frustrations of the practical man have practical remedies, but those of the thoughtful egoist who has questioned the competence of time to furnish him with satisfaction entail remedies which are constitutional and philosophic. One can always withdraw from a situation with which one is not identified. Indeed, the accidental is not a neutral or impersonal fact, but is disclosed in this very reserve of the individual who is not ready to settle for the arbitrary and ephemeral as the center and actuality of his own existence. Anyone, then, who does not find time constitutional and self-definitive must look elsewhere. He must look before and after and pine for what is not. The romantic soul is aware of a schism that is more than a disappointment over his investments in the market. Mistrust of time expresses no calm and tentative pondering of the superior advantages of refraining from giving hostages to fortune while sensibly pursuing one's purpose in other more profitable ways.

It is not easy, then, to divest oneself of time and to renounce all interest in it, even if one wanted to. Nor is this difficulty plausibly ascribed to the allurements and seductions of natural objects and to the weakness of the flesh, as if a man's lower nature subverted his higher faculties into eating his dinner, dragging him down to an interest in learning, to a nice competence in his craft, to honest solvency in his enterprise, or to love of a woman. Neither are these activities under the direction of timeless perfection, as if a person in no way identified with eating and drinking, in no close intimacy with books and politics, viewing them all from a superior distance, decided for no earthly reason that he would like some tea and toast. Such a plunge into the concrete could only be regarded as a miracle. This estranging dualism suggests an ability to weigh time against the timeless as if the discriminating shopper, who reads a consumers' magazine, were identified with neither. And so one is led to wonder where one stands when recommending so absolute a preference or when apportioning the proper measure of concern in each. What is the apparatus of this judgment? And, for that matter, why make the choice at all?

It is an overlooked property of choice that one can always decline the gambit. If you ask me whether I wish to go to Boston or to New York this weekend, I may decide to stay home, satisfied with what I have. To urge a choice between good and evil is to imply a possible indifference to the distinction, and the more portentous the choice is made to appear, the more one may be inclined to cultivate one's cabbages in tranquility. What is more, the consequence of a choice is untrustworthy. Tomorrow's newspaper, the latest book, the word of a friend, may lead one to think that one has been hasty in the balancing of advantages. It is worth noting, too, that choices lose importance and clarity when not operating as the implementation of resolve. Indifference does not choose. Before Caesar, many had crossed the Rubicon, but they had not cast the die. Choices are tentative, not absolutely but with respect to the resolve that sets the stage for their urgency and for their intelligent propriety. Choice, after all, is not on the loose but is restricted by the self-identifying functioning of an actual person. There it finds its occasion, its necessity, its specific tentativeness, and its intelligent modification in the sequel of particular experiences. Only so can it then be said that the choice was either wise or incautious.

The persistent and eloquent mistrust of time strongly suggests that we are not here dealing with some accidental item of experience. Time poses a problem of one's identity and nobody wishes to be identified with unessentials. So long as we viewed temporal change as a region in which mind and individuality were not to be discovered, we could properly bewail its mutability, seeking for ourselves a steadier reality beyond unstable fortune or laying hold of some untroubled hour of inconsequential pleasure. But historians, perhaps with more enthusiasm than deliberation, have concerned themselves with the past as if with materials in which the character of man had been revealed—as if, like other scholars, they controlled some way of telling a coherent story about a distinctive factor of experience.

It was not until the record of acts had been set down in documents and these had been accepted as genuine disclosures that the identification of our own actuality with time and deeds acquired not only plausibility but a powerful authority. We grew into our past without prior deliberation, without philosophic sanction, and then found that we had no way of accrediting a dimension of learning that contained all that we had ever done, all that we had ever thought, and all that had given occasion for our specific actuality. Then for the first time we could turn upon this pretender to knowledge and ask for credentials. There was not much to offer. Our ideals have been timeless and ahistoric. They offered no constitutional authority to time but sought rather to coerce it into subordination to the immutable.

The old and traditional mistrust of time has not, in short, resulted from some defect of history, for there has been no constitutional structure to the past. History was not so much a defective mode of experience as no formal mode whatsoever. The past, and therefore the present that had generated it, stood together as manifestations of psychology. What we said was opinion; what we did was impulse. We could learn about particulars and acquire useful skills, satisfying an irrational propensity. Our skill in warfare has been considerable, but the preservation or extension of individual power has been ascribed to an instinct of pugnacity or aggression, backed by other drives and urges such as sex or food hunger. On a social scale war has been declared a manifestation of tribalism, beset with prejudice of race or creed, and obviously nothing that a person not victimized by nature would undertake. The political liberal has wondered on what basis he could declare himself and take a stand, since action abandoned the felicity of a critical aloofness, brought down upon one a partisanship that suspended an evenhanded deliberation, and put one in the uncomfortable position of being observed by the superior person as no better than any other psychological oddity. Absolutism in all its forms reflects an unwillingness to be identified with finitude in its opinions and desires. And so we have vacillated between the high absorptions of the moment and the repudiation of all such deceptive sufficiencies. If history is psychology, then the modes of the accidental take charge of it and explain it.

The alternative has been the ahistoric, beliefs not proposed or proved by experience, acts not motivated by circumstance, morality that sees defeat in any alliance with our finitude. One need but read the daily paper to find evidence of the scope of this intimidating absolutism, as when, for example, political rights are talked about as if they had a sanction in the arcane depths of the individual, and owed nothing to the actual community of resolute men or to that long and arduous career of our essays in functional interdependence. These attitudes are themselves the revelations of time. No one mistrusts what he has not embraced and found wanting in terms of its own pretentions. Psychology cannot recommend "adjustment to the environment" and then elevate our adaptations into finalities. Engulfing desires come to no enduring satisfaction in the accidental, and accidental desires pass with no more reason than authorized their arrival. It is not history that we have repudiated, but prehistoric and dissociated moments.

History made its appearance in a world that the most responsible thought of man had already shaped into various modes of unity and order. Change, multiplicity, and the fierce concentrations of finitude had all seemed deficient in that universality and stability which bespoke the disinterested reason of man and the integrity of his world. It came as something of a shock that the rationality that we had cherished had had a career. It was even worse to entertain the idea that without the career there could be no rationality that we could identify as our own. These considerations were slow in making themselves felt. There persisted, and still persists, the attempt to bring history under some alien unity. There was the record of what men had done and said, but what sense did it make and how were we to call that "knowledge" which lacked a rule of unity? How was history to be brought under the classic pattern of the ahistoric cognitive ideal?

Peculiar faculties not themselves caught in time had to be invoked as the implements of criticism. An aloof "reason" was to preside over thought, and a supervising "conscience" over every wish and every act, over all our undertakings and institutions, over all mortal emergencies. The warders of our finitude, if there were to be any, were necessarily not themselves part of our own cumulative experience. The universal in the object appeared as the consequence of the universal in the subject. When, as with the psychological empiricists, no universality could be found in our own experience, none could be attributed to the objects of experience. But if we ourselves can employ an innate universal, then the rational ideal discloses its nontemporal character in the very equation between ourselves and our nontemporal faculties. The rule of order led to powers within us that for their own satisfaction demanded analogous powers beyond us. And so we looked behind, beneath, above, all the shifting changes of time for a constancy which complemented our own demands. The gaze of man was to be directed—could not avoid being directed—toward foundations not actually in sight or toward a splendid superstructure never to be reached by the measured gradation of a continuous approach. It has seemed, indeed, that the force of the cognitive ideal must carry beyond all possible mutability. It was a major moment in the life of reason when the security of the grand object of thought failed to establish itself in the actual, so that a superlative reality, an *ens realissimum,* had to be accepted as the guarantee of the eventual order of any present event. To be quite pure, reason had to lead on to a situation which stood apart from whatever happened. The timeless universal could not consort with time. It could not be part of history.

Given the problem of order as one of unity, and given diversity and change as the helplessness of understanding, what would one do if not project into its ultimate consequences such organization as we already possessed? Certainly no one concerned with history could fail to be sympathetic to these formidable essays. But no one interested in history can renew absolutism by dispensing judgments of true and false. He would disqualify history in that gesture of intellectual superiority. In history we cannot disavow what we have done or said. It is not merely a question of ignoring or denying what took place; it is rather that the past act is a progenitor of the present, a

10

Alliance with Time

If one uses words one is allied with time and with the past. No word makes sense in the present tense. It means now what it has come to mean, so the unabridged dictionary can run to many volumes. We live, too, in a legal order where a rule of law contains earlier interpretations now modified or sharpened. Lawyers cite cases that once were the specific occasions of disputed meanings. When not arbitrary, the law takes time. The affections, too, need time for the disclosure of their solidity and power as well as for their impulsiveness or mutability. A nation takes time to establish its unity, its character and its aims, its capacities and its frailties. In all these instances the past appears as the necessary condition of a present action. No man can tell what he is doing or what he is saying if he has not already acted and spoken. Nor can that be discovered by another where act and word are no part of a continuum reaching into the past.

While involved in the processes of time, we are, and have been, reluctant to grant them authority. The past has often been felt as a bondage. "The wisdom and the folly of ages speaks constantly in us," says Huizinga. "Time and again there are those to whom it seems as if history is suffocating us all." Feeling may seem inhibited by established custom. To use the right word entails the delay and, perhaps, the clogging confusion of deliberation. We long for Arcady—"a shepherd I, a shepherd he." It is a difficult matter to attend the university and not lose simplicity in the learned proprieties. Rabelais presents a version of the ahistoric ideal in his remarkable pleasure dome, the Abbey of Thélème, where everyone walked in elegant refinement and no one was quickened by those risky energies that generate problems and uncertainties. There a gallant and a lady might fall in love, but once married they lived elsewhere, as Rabelais blandly relates. One still reads occasionally about a person who, like Henry Thoreau, refuses to pay taxes, mistrusting the institutions and purposes for which public money is spent or, perhaps, agreeing with certain statesmen that expenditure is more wise and efficient when the self-reliant man does his own shopping around for schools and drinking water. In many ways the processes and institutions that take time have appeared as a threat to the autonomy of the moment. Nor would one be able to deny that the past can shackle the present, although when the sense of constraint is strong, it is because some particular aspect of life has changed from what it was, and so has come into conflict with another and static element of politics or thought.

A chronological past that is throughout no more than an earlier version of the present furnishes no suggestion of constraint. And a novelty that can pretend to nothing but difference with an arbitrary heritage has no better claim to acceptance. The past, if it has become repressive in some aspects, must furnish its own grounds of reform if the change is to have the articulate sanction. Saint Paul drew quotations from the older prophets, even though he also said, "But now we are discharged from the law, dead to that which held us captive, so that we serve not under the old written code but in the new life of the Spirit." Except for anarchists, time retains a hesitant prestige. Education struggles with this problem, especially in the humanities, where concern with the past is unavoidable.

Using the current idiom one might say that attitudes toward the past are "ambiguous." But what we confront here is no verbal slipperiness or uncertainty of particular purposes. We face rather a fateful conflict in the interpretation of our world. The disparagement of time is no fitful impulse. It draws its strength from the orthodox and traditional background of our most systematic thought. This ahistoric ideal Ortega calls Eleatic, from the city of Elea, in southern Italy, where there appeared a number of men who argued with originality and brilliance that change was illusion and not reality. To Elea there came from Colophon, in Asia Minor, the philosopher Xenophanes about 540 B.C. He was a monotheist who rejected the current anthropomorphic view of the gods. "But mortals suppose that the gods are born (as they themselves are) and that they wear men's clothing and have human voice and body." Anticipating Plato, he says further, "Homer and Hesiod attributed to the gods all things which are disreputable and worthy of blame when done by men." A second and more celebrated figure was Parmenides. He says of the One Being, "It is unmoved, in the hold of great chains, without beginning or end since generation and destruction have completely disappeared, and true belief has rejected them. It lies the same, abiding in the same state, and by itself . . . but it is lacking in nothing." As everyone knows, it was Zeno the Eleatic who contended that Achilles, the swift-footed, the goddess-born, could not really overtake the slow-coach tortoise once the plodding reptile had, incautiously, been allowed a start in a foot race. It stood to reason, argued Zeno, that one could not additively exhaust the infinite. And, since the real is the rational, motion, which entails infinity even in its briefest extent, could only be the illusion of appearance, and no reality. In our day, Henri Bergson and Bertrand Russell have not thought it anachronistic to address themselves to this annoying problem, although for very different reasons and with dissimilar results—Russell, like a good Eleatic, still trying to be rational, and Bergson associating motion with vitalism and its immediacies.

Reason unifies; so it was believed. To be quite rational was, then, to propose in one form or another a single substance, being, or process in which all plurality is dissolved. No literate man in the Western world lacks acquaintance with this way of interpreting experience. Philosophy began as the cult of rationality. There is a story about Thales of Miletus, in Asia Minor, which tells that when he had at last brought a problem in geometry to a solution he went to the altar of his house and made grateful sacrifice to the god. Why should he not, indeed, as a majestic universality loomed about him? This was no longer Miletus, it was a world, and he himself the individual whose pure and formal thought had penetrated to universality and so to infinity. Mathematicians from Thales and Protagoras to our own day have felt this emancipation from time and change. "Euclid alone has looked on beauty bare." The logicians, or some of them, also claim that their order holds sway in all possible worlds, and owes nothing to this one: quite a large saying, if one stops to think of it, rather breath-taking in fact, since breathing, a biological accident, has nothing to do with it and never appears as a postulate on page one. "There be two men of all mankind / That I'm forever thinking on," sang Edwin Arlington Robinson: "They chase me everywhere I go— / Melchizedek, Ucalegon." Like these two, mathematics and logic are sometimes said to lack mortal ancestors and to be without legitimate progeny. And this is considered creditable. The rest is an accidental and psychological multiplicity upon which it is necessary to impose an alien logical structure.

The knowledge which is also power discloses the nature of things. Hammers drive nails, and petrol drives pistons, as practical control demonstrates. Purposes can be neither formulated nor executed without reliable sequences in nature. If, as Emerson says, nature is what I may do, then accomplishment reflects regularity among objects while objects gain precision through purposed control. In the end, when naturalism has become absolute, having forgotten the base degrees by which it has risen, it may seem, and it has seemed, that purpose must vanish into the uniformities that first found discovery and recommendation through its own activity. To know the causes of things may be to lose the name of action when the absolute order is no longer a function of the finite energies without which its particular ways get no exploration and convey no value. The idea that power lies in knowledge becomes "demonic" when knowledge engulfs all that we are and do. Man becomes an object and his ways can be formulated.

It is only a question of the scope of our information. John Stuart Mill finds oddities and irregularities in conduct, such as were formerly found in an undeveloped astronomy or in the description of tides. Much of what is known about man remains statistical although "it is evidently possible to make predictions which will *almost* always be verified." For a proper "science of Human Nature" he wants something more. "But in order to give a genuinely scientific character to the study it is indispensable that these approximate generalizations, which in themselves would amount only to the lowest kind of empirical laws, should be connected deductively with the laws from which they result; should be resolved into the properties on which the phenomena depend." This is Eleaticism in the guise of empiricism, stalking through the world seeking what it can devour.

There must be few men educated in the past fifty years who have not encountered the hope that knowledge might attain a sweep in which all but a few odds and ends had been included. This seductive vision is not to be scorned. It is the application of ancient rationalism to empirical multiplicity and to the quest of man for power. Except for miracles, nature is now acknowledged by all as an intelligible order. The strength of this conviction does not rest on inductive generalization but on the concepts and symbols of quantitative order.

11

A Victory Is in Time

If in Eden there was no guilt, neither had there been an act. The Christian story took the form of exhibiting in time not so much the repudiation of time as its acceptance. This is the price of the pretension to have acted. But the act needs also to express its independence of all finite cause and consequence if it is not to fall back into a control other than its own.

The historical event that was central for Augustine was also a victory over time, although it did not repudiate time. It was in time because it established dates. We still write B.C. and A.D. There is no need to adopt just this point of departure. One could date in terms of A.U.C.—from the founding of the city of Rome. In any case one has to date from an event related to an act. This act, in turn, can be any sort of act, but it is always something more than an event in nature. There are no dates in test tubes or in logic, mathematics, or physics. Sciences have histories, but only in terms of the sayings, doings, or observations which have made some discovery memorable. Nor is it the case that dates are calmly assigned to events of importance, as if one knew all along what was important and then selected one such event as the point of departure. One's birthday may not be the moment in time from which one proceeds to an understanding of one's life. Perhaps it was rather that one day one set out for Damascus, or looked into Chapman's Homer, or sustained a bewildering reverse. One then looks backward and forward. Dates require the human factor. This is not to say, either, that they are psychological. Action moves out of psychology into the existent. The question is, Has one managed to do just that? Nobody can make the claim except in so far as somewhere he pretends to a finality. It is where we have taken ourselves in hand in terms of a previous condition that we reckon the emergence of our actuality. One could approach the problem of history in terms of the question, How is action disclosed to us?

So long as the ideal remains remote and without illustration, it can furnish no contrast of good and evil within the limits of experience and of life. This was a problem troublesome to Plato, who wanted to define justice and other qualities apart from alleged examples. He wanted to find a man who, although to all appearances unjust, and so liable to every sort of injury, was really just and prepared to face an inimical world. But justice nowhere illustrated leaves injustice also unexemplified. This was likewise the peculiarity of Cartesian skepticism; mistrust had no basis in any actual criterion. No actual case of deception could be exhibited.

Time cannot be wholly repudiated when it becomes the medium in which the soul is identified. The troubles that permitted men to realize that they were "lost" express a finitude partly self-conscious. Presumably the animals that Adam had named also had to live in some other place than Paradise, but one does not hear that they have blamed either God or demons or themselves, or that they have lamented their estate or groped for salvation. They never acted, never alienated the eternal by embracing time. The frustrations of time were not specific but constitutional. They were formal and existential, not local or psychological, the frustrations not of a purpose but of will itself. Self-direction was frustrated in so far as no absolute dwelt in the will and defined it. And so Paul cried out, "But I see in my members another law." And he said, "I do not understand my own actions. For I do not do what I want, but I do the very thing I hate." This is the frustration of the

egoist who can't act. What is there to be found in himself
that he can't repudiate? How will he escape an alien law
that either surges up in the natural man or else rebukes
those spontaneities as sinful? The answer he gave was in
terms of "charity," a disposition of the will, yet regulative.
The authority for this lay in the actuality of a will that,
though incorporate, had defined itself in the new formu-
lation of all finite aims. Let them serve the disinterested.
But the disinterested could be exhibited only in a passionate act that involved the relinquishment of specific finite
purposes while expressing the very life that embodied
them. Paul's problems descended to Augustine, and these
two egoists have the same answer.

It rates observation that these events are of a formal sort.
Although actual, they do not depend on specific truths, or
on truths at all. They deal only in the constitution of the
will. When they are represented as "facts" they become
magical. That morality is formal is a view much assailed,
largely on the ground that it would not then tell us what
to do next. As well expect geometry to tell the volume of
the Parthenon, or numbers to furnish the population of
Afghanistan, or logic to say "who done it." It is the standing confusion between will and purpose that is responsible
for this sort of argument. Will is the form of purposes.
Paul and Augustine give witness of the decay of purposes
where they lack form—that is, where action is not defined
in principle. In our time this leads to the psychiatric couch,
the place where will is disorganized and lost. If the difficulty of formalism occurs in a lack of connection with particular purposes, the ethics of purpose gives no account of
how one could act at all. Jonathan Edwards, the American
Calvin, had to supplement the psychology of choice with
forces of good and evil that controlled what a man would
think of himself as one who chose. The way of purpose
always takes the "greatest apparent good," but the *real*
good, which consists in the comprehension of all apparent
goods, has a different and transcendent status, and is
revealed through no experience open to finitude. No more
of course is evil. This is not the psychology of action, but

of the passive, a temper for which Edwards found support in John Locke, whose theory of knowledge, being psychological, exhibits the same absence of any actual criterion. Locke himself was expressing in most delicate style the temper of a passive empiricism, in that limbo which is neither heaven nor hell and there awaits deliverance. Action always vanishes where finitude is not constitutional. Action, though the advertisement of limit, did, through the very sense of guilt and frustration, discover its own present authority. If the rule of the intellect is the maintenance of the conditions of error, so too the rule of the will is the maintenance of its own capacity for guilt. The actual is the locus of the assertion and maintenance of these distinctions. It is the individual, the other absolute, of which all articulate infinity is the form.

The only universal in man is his individuality, and this is the other infinity. It is tied to time and to guilt. To declare himself an agent, Adam had no option but to confront the sole rival absolute. The modern parallel would occur if a behaviorist were treasonously to separate himself from nature and defy it by eating an apple. "Do I dare to eat a peach? / I shall wear white flannel trousers, and walk upon the beach."

Time, then, appears as the locus both of finitude and of an infinity. What conveyed the infinity was identification with time in an act, but an act which expressed no temporal purpose. Error, like wrong, requires a past tense. An ethics of the present, like a logic of the present, has nothing to be set right. One can do without them, never having done anything. A present not identified in its past has no deficiencies. Egoism is the assertion of the moment as the actuality of time. It is the redemption of time. Time becomes the region of our exile in the very act that implies that time is one of the modes of infinity. We have a stake in guilt, a metaphysical stake, one that speaks not of transcendence, but of actuality.

12

The Sense of Time

Nature without time is hardly worth considering, even if one allows for no more than the science of mechanics. Change is not so much time-consuming as time-expressing. Time is not quite "the measure of motion," as Aristotle said, but rather part of its meaning. Without a clock, it would be difficult to study physics, where motion is incessant and so not mortal.

An earlier feeling for time centered on mortality rather than on the incessant. The monasteries observed the "hours" from matins to complin. Nature was overshadowed by life, and life by its finitude. To this day the mortality of man seems axiomatic and is used in the major premise of an illustrative syllogism, as if it were a statement both familiar and secure, a proper basis for the exhibition of a logical consequence. It was in this context of man's state, rather than that of natural knowledge, that Augustine considered time. His *Confessions* still rates as a biography of the first order, profound in its honesty and intense in its feeling. He, of course, was deeply involved with time, for it was the scene of his guilt and exile.

For Augustine time is but the vestibule of eternity. "What then is time?" he asks in the *Confessions*. "If no one asks me I know, if I wish to explain it to one that asks I know not: yet I say boldly that I know that if nothing passed away time past was not. But the present, should it always be present, and never pass into time past, verily it should not be time, but eternity."

"The world was made with time, and not in time," he says. "No time passed before the world, because no creature was made by whose course it might pass." Time emerges from the timeless. It is a property of the creature of the Eternal. As for that Eternal Being, "His knowledge is not as ours is, admitting alteration by circumstance of time, but exempted from all change and all variation of moments. All things he knows are present at the same time in his spiritual vision." For Augustine, as for Kant, true being does not age. It is ahistoric.

The absolutism of Augustine could hardly be exceeded. He will not allow Plato to ascribe to the creator any gratification over the wonderful universe that he has composed. The reference is to the *Timaeus,* where Plato says, "When the father and creator saw the creature which he made moving and living, the created image of the eternal gods, he rejoiced, and in his joy determined to make the copy still more like the original; and as this was eternal, he sought to make the universe eternal so far as might be. . . . Wherefore he resolved to have a moving image of eternity . . . and this image we call time." Augustine says, however, "He was so foolish as to think that the newness of the work increased God's joy," an emotional deviation from the imperturbable serenity of the divine. In *Genesis,* God also saw that it was good; but Augustine hastens to explain that "He teaches, but learns not, that it is good." God can't learn anything, not even from what he has made. Creation is no evolution of the divine experience. "All things he knows are present at the same time in his spiritual vision." No clearer picture of the ahistoricity of Augustine's absolute could be furnished.

We, in contrast, cannot escape history. We cannot disavow our acts and our partiality if we are to learn. Indeed, there is no point to learning from what has been done unless the deed is the manifestation of limit, corrected by the intention which launched it, and exhibiting that intention in both its energy and its incompleteness. We must learn from what has been done. Good and evil appear apropos of that.

Plato's world is not so explicitly closed as Augustine's. Plato never quite capitulated to "father Parmenides." The life of reason is haunted by the "other," as well as by the "same," by multiplicity and relation as well as by unity, by aspiring passion as well as by the ecstatic vision. But Augustine set the tone for much that was to follow, and the success of the derogation of time bears witness to our inability to endow it with authority. To lapse into the technical: finitude has not been viewed as a "category"—that is, as an essential factor of being; it has lacked "ontological" status. It has been derivative, a creature, a dependent. Its solicitations, therefore, are usurpers. The world, the flesh, and the devil are to be renounced. This is the situation in which history becomes a heresy. Much, indeed most, of Western philosophy—as well, of course, as most of Oriental thought—is a corollary of this mistrust of time and finitude. Once *ancilla theologiae,* philosophy is now *ancilla scientiae.* Kant's soul was filled with awe by "the starry heavens above, and the moral law within," two loci of immense and compulsive orders immune to change and opinion. The avidity with which the timeless has been sought out, in both logic and morals, bears witness to the neglect of the historical.

There occurs, however, in Augustine one massive exception to the eternal poise. It is, of course, a mystery, but it is essential. This is the Incarnation. In spite of *Ecclesiastes* there can be something new under the sun, something unique, not repetitive, not a "case" of a universal, not a logical particular, but individual and therefore blazing with a new importance. "For Christ once died for our sins, and rising again, does no more, nor hath death any future dominion over him." Here one sees the central difference between nature and the individual. The individual is, in principle, not a case, not an instance, not repetitive. He is himself and not something else. Time becomes associated with eternity in so far as it is not to be understood through nature or through the reason appropriate to the invariant and anonymous. "The Word was made flesh, and dwelt among us." One is well advised not to treat this as mere "superstition." It is, of course, as Paul said, "to the Jews a stumbling block, and to the Greeks a scandal." But this only goes to show how difficult it is for us to associate reason and the unique. The philosophy of history is an essay in the rationality that does not exclude the unique—that is, the act—and the moment. "If in yourself you cannot break a spring, beware how much you compress it," wrote F. H. Bradley in his *Aphorisms*. This spring has taken a lot of compression, but the appearance of existentialism is evidence that it has not been broken. If Augustine forsook time it was because of an affirmation that appeared in time, plucking safety from the nettle danger. The redemption has its transcendent features; it seems perverse to neglect the one element that gave it persuasion, namely, the transformation of time by the actuality of the unique, and so of something infinite. This has been at once the core and the ferment in the Christian doctrine. It is awkward to have "theories" about the unique, to turn the hose of common sense on the pentecostal flame.

13

Time and Immediacy

The sense of time is a primitive idea and appears without benefit of theory. One could hardly plan to have a past, or predict that, in view of long experience, there was every likelihood of finding one in the not too remote future. Time is an immediacy, but one that expands and moves into diversity and relation. The present is no more articulate than its temporal environment, and today without its own yesterdays lacks temporal distinction. Although primitive, it preserves no fixity and generates no merely "analytic" consequences, but rather the novel and unanticipated.

An elementary, and perhaps the first, encounter with time occurs in psychological learning and memory. There was a time when one could not drive a car, or move on skis. Now, perhaps, one can, and one remembers trials and errors. This sort of past is two-sided. There is the greater knowledge about the effects of specific acts in terms of the properties of objects—autos and skis and all the other objects with which they operate. There are also the changes in the operator—confidence, skill, readiness, sociability, docility, annoyance, sharpened observation, control, and much else. The common denominator is an action, not a passive perception—not, one may say, a "logical construction placed upon sense data." There is likely to be muscle in it. Indeed, memory has been elusive when looked for in passivity. No one can say where the perceptual blue begins and the remembered blue ends, so far as the color is concerned, a point that has troubled a psychological empiricism that can't do without memory. Learning involves the redefinition of objects in terms of action, and what one remembers is no isolated sensation or fact, but the previous experience in an enlarged and connected setting. One now remembers that one used to find it hard to keep to the outer edge of the road, or to gauge distance and rate, provided however that such awkwardness had come to one's attention apropos of an effort to drive safely and without alarming the passengers. Memory is a factor of control, not of passivity. Nor would there be any occasion to remember apart from the needs of a present exertion. It is action that holds distinct the present and the past, even as it also brings them together. There is no cognition without function, whether the cognition be a perception or a memory.

This sort of time is not, however, historical time. Nor is such learning the study of history. Historians of all sorts need be no more skillful than other people, and one may, in fact, feel as safe with a chauffeur or with a licensed navigator. Psychological learning is concerned with the simultaneous region of experience with its rules and laws. In that region it breeds skill, control, recognition.

Hesiod writes about the farmer's year, and offers very applicable recommendations for planting, harvesting, sailing, and other economic concerns. His past experience relates, however, to no other age or mentality, to no other set of circumstances than those which were then present. Next year, too, one will do well to watch for the crane flying south and then start one's plowing, and when the cicada sings it will be time to seek shade and lessen labor. All that, he has learned, and now as a farmer remembers. But in these practical discernments there is no question of the fatality of the artifactual world, no problem of time itself in the life of man, no suggestion that we live in history as well as in the procession of the seasons. Hesiod was, of course, something besides a farmer, and he wrote about the five ages of the world, about events which he had never experienced and never could. In this he illustrates a dawning historical sense. For history began as myth. But in giving advice to farmers and sailors he was talking about what he had learned in the simultaneous and contemporary world.

The sense of time finds a place in many philosophical accounts of our knowledge of nature. Aristotle listed it among the "categories," the most general modes of discourse and of knowledge. A modern instance is furnished by Immanuel Kant. The intimacy of time with our experience was for him so close and indissoluble that he declared time to be *a priori,* not derived from specific experiences, but rather their condition. He called it an intuition, something directly apprehended. "An intuition is *a priori* if it contains nothing but the form of sensibility, antedating in the mind all the actual impressions through which I am affected by objects." The intimacy of time with experience, especially with finite experience, is not usually denied, but that it be an *a priori* connection among all impressions, and a formal element among objects of nature, has occasioned severe criticism. This is not because the *a priori* is nowadays quite in disgrace; far from it. It is because there is objection to any foreclosure of the properties of objects. And Kant was talking about objects quite as much as about sensibility. His categories were the common denominator of objects and of their apprehension. He was not proposing that we came upon time as if by accident, perhaps to our surprise or to our annoyance. There was no surprise involved, no neutral point of view to which the sense of time would be adventitious. This, then, was the immediacy of time, its intimacy and authority. Accidental features of experience could be warily scrutinized, but this scrutiny occurred in terms of the *a priori* modes of order to which the accidental conformed.

Kant did not, of course, claim that time was "real," or that it "existed." It was one of the shapes of experience and of nature as experienced. That side of Kant has also been much assailed. There are many who object to being too intimate with nature, and for the very reason that Kant's position proclaimed, namely, that intimacy can pass over into identity. Kant did not claim to know about time; he knew objects in terms of time. To know about time is to leave it adventitious, like the planet Pluto, so that one isn't closely involved with it, but can talk about it with detached logic, adopt attitudes of approval or aversion, or perhaps direct one's attention elsewhere to more edifying concerns. Chesterton said that he despised the solar system, and perhaps it does leave something to be desired, what with our cold winters and hot summers, but to do without time was for Kant to abolish the solar system and all the stars and milky ways.

The *a priori* of Kant was introduced not in order to evade empiricism, but rather to establish it. The "logical construction placed upon sense data," an expression of the logical positivists, operates in much the same way as Kant's *a priori*. It makes intellectual sense out of qualitative sense. What Kant said was only that when one perceived any quality, one did so in a context. He said that no discrete quality was an absolute, no island was sufficient unto itself. Natural science, he thought, organized its data apropos of time not because time imposed an alien formality, but because succession was an unavoidable constituent of every identification. The intimacy of time to the perceiver was only the other side of its intimacy with whatever was perceived. As an "inner sense" not reflected in the outer apprehension, its inwardness would be no better than any superstition. He wished to save and establish the order of nature, the region of knowledge, not the inner sense of time as a sort of conscientious scruple. Indeed, it is often made a point against Kant that he gave no account of an individual moment of perception, but talked about perception in general, *Bewusstsein überhaupt*. His "synthetic judgments *a priori*" were drained of all psychology. A reaction against him occurred precisely over this anonymous impersonality of experience.

It was this impersonality in Kant, or anywhere else, that gave to time, for all its immediacy, only an intellectual status. No moment possessed the urgency and desperation of one's own actuality. It summoned to thought, not to action. Existentialism began as a revolt against such impersonality, against the insignificance of the moment when its role was restricted to perception. An early, although often neglected, example occurs in Fichte. The feeling of romantic urgency is the theme of *The Vocation of Man,* where an escape is attempted from nature whether as reality or as phenomenon. Kant arrested spontaneity in the name of the law. His temper was severe. He made no concessions to finitude, and even his moral doctrine (and it was a thing of splendor) made of virtue a sort of reason and consistency. No doubt it must be so; but the point of emphasis in Kant was not that consistency had no actuality apart from its operation in relative disorder, and as the self-maintenance of such disorder. In his time nature and reason were the chief loci of human freedom, and the messy improvisation and desperate affirmation of concrete situations seemed as yet no part of man's dignity and power.

In this quarter one finds the ahistoricity of Kant's idea of time. He declared it primitive and immediate, but intellectual. The intellectually primitive is very likely to turn up as something *a priori,* as a code or a rule, as a postulate or convention. Indeed, every effort is still made to rescue such formal elements of experience from the taint of the accidental. And in these efforts, because they are accounts of cognition, time and the other categories lose their finite actuality. Must not the governors of what could be otherwise claim immunity to the here and now? It is an old and an appealing claim. But it is ahistoric. Time's transformations are discredited. The intellectual idea, and even the moral ideal, have found in time an elusive enemy not to be subdued by disregard nor yet capable of being viewed as a passing accident within finitude. And so time is appropriated by the universal and becomes an ironic vehicle of the ahistoric itself.

It should be understood that in these observations nothing censorious is intended. Of Kant's great essay we may say, "We do it wrong, being so majestical, to offer it the show of violence." The sense of time can be revealed only in its frustrations, and these, in turn, cannot appear until they have been formulated. Kant addressed himself to nature, not to history. It is for this reason that cognition became shrouded in noumena. The local stands in the universal and lacks systematic force of its own when the actual and the finite are not made constitutional. Recent disparagements of metaphysics, launched in the interests of a purified cognition, have shifted the locus of the ahistoric, but have not abandoned it. From all this we may be confident that whatever we say about cognition, it will possess some factor of ahistoric universality, perhaps as logic or as mathematics. But whether these universals can themselves be clarified except as the form of finite actuality is a further question. It is a question in the philosophy of history.

It would, however, be a very serious matter to look for time apart from nature. There has been a marked vagrancy in post-Kantian egoisms such as one finds in the existentialists. Nature has the enormous advantage of being an area of discipline and of community. Take it away and the modern mind would collapse into the primitive. Even morality needs a medium, a content which enforces a decent respect for the opinion of mankind, an objectified self-criticism to which every man may be held as he lives and breathes and eats his supper, as he is the child of parents who supplied nurture and a conquered environment. The time of nature is not the only form of time, but it is one of its defining forms. And for this disclosure, organized and architectural, we go to Kant. And, if we no longer build in that style, it is graceless to forget its arresting announcement.

14

The Sense of History

We are now a long way from nature in the raw. We work with tools and machines that science and technology have produced. We earn a living in the marketplace and do not drink from springs or hunt for meat or barter for commodities. We are affected by decisions taken east of Suez. Our stimuli to thought and action occur apropos of objects which have, for the most part, been made by man: a house, a room, a book, picture, song, a spoken word. Our dress for the day may be determined by a look at a barometer or thermometer, or by hearing the weather forecast over the radio. We buy insurance based on intricate actuarial calculations that only the mathematician can perform. Our civil law is defined in courts, made in legislatures, proclaimed at Runnymede or Philadelphia. We actually do, or think, very little except under the stimulus and control of what has already been done and thought.

All this surrounds us inescapably. Excitement and restraint invoke the same medium. To speak is to give hostages to grammar and to an appropriate logic. When we vacation in the woods, we carry more or less of the equipment of civilization, perhaps even a book, and it takes a few awkward days before we learn to look more sharply at weather signs, or to speak less and lower in a new and strange environment. Our world is our own. It is what we have made it to be.

There occurs also a more or less vague feeling that the

artifactual world not only surrounds us but has ways of its own, that it harbors a "fate," and that the house one lives in is not a neutral object that serves one's passing purposes, but has effects upon one for good or ill. Nor can one establish institutions like the state and say that "all men are created equal" and then be done with it. Such declarations, embodied in institutions, make unexpected exactions in terms of politics, economics, education, and manners.

The nemesis of free institutions lies in their enforcement of a position of consequence upon every man. Such institutions can be established only by ourselves, and at hazard. The world of daily living is inevitably made our own, and this fact looms before us and requires acknowledgment. It brings home to us the sense of forces and consequences that were unsuspected and, very likely, unwanted. Every essay at control invokes a nemesis. When we shrink from these involvements and hazards, as well we may, we can spare ourselves disappointments only at the price of an annihilative inaction.

If history embodied no fatality it would become an intellectual oddity, and one could have a look at it or not, as best suited one's temperament or practical aims. It is not unusual to find history weakly recommended as a "cultural" subject or more strongly proposed as a "practical" aid, perhaps in diplomacy. It might be thought that one could talk about history in a detached mood, as if history were a phenomenon to be observed with disinterested calm. Instead, one finds that one has introduced the idea of fate, or contrasted time with eternity or history with ahistoric modes of experience, or in some other way has introduced disturbing ideas. One deals with things done, *res gestae,* with acts rather than facts, with yesterday rather than with an invariant present, with rise and fall and not with quantitative changes of objects in time and space. The ideal of natural knowledge is the disinterested, the understanding of the ways of things in despite of our hopes and fears. But action, with which history is concerned, is the expression of hopes and fears and is not to be understood by us apart from our personal appropriation of their occasions. If we do not do this, we are not fitted to understand. History can show us only ourselves, for it is our deed. But it is also a deed that continues into the present and so cannot be forsaken or interrupted. It is not a romantic tale or a tale told by an idiot, for it is the story which contains the genesis of all such distinctions. We cannot escape it, because it is ourselves. And this makes us uncomfortable and may even seem to disqualify it as a proper region of inquiry.

Are we not to leave ourselves out of the picture where we claim any sort of knowledge? And if there is a true knowledge of man, must it not be offered in terms of nature, of body, stimulus, response, and objectively ascertained learning? To answer such questions in the affirmative is to deny that history can be an autonomous dimension of experience. There we cannot leave ourselves out of the picture or treat an act as if it were an odd sort of fact. Indeed, what passes for "fact" is itself variable in time and has only a historical force. Nor could one overlook the possibility—and it has been asserted—that the facts depend upon active inquiry, and even upon what will satisfy us. Nevertheless, the idea that history finds one in a reflective attitude may well cause misgivings.

Historians themselves are much given to the facts, even when they say that their facts are acts. The Parthenon is a sort of fact, but it was built by the Greeks, a peculiar race—by Athenians—in the fifth century B.C., and it was a shrine for Athena, a divine personage whose statue by Phidias it housed. It would be difficult to say one had seen the Parthenon unless, in a manner of speaking, one could make some sense out of Athena, who was, no doubt, a pagan idol, and never existed in heaven or earth. There is no Parthenon as a matter of fact, but it does impress one as a rather formidable historical monument. No artifact can be discovered in intellectual passivity. It is no datum, but a factum, something done.

We discover our human estate in a world of our own doing. It is a region disclosed only by reflection. We cannot escape these reflections.

Historical events are not to be judged by ahistoric criteria. We are accustomed to argue and to criticize, and we
usually cherish standards of appraisal that guide statements
and acts. Rightly so, but in so far as we employ a fixed
measure, we only illustrate a position in the changes of
time; we do not make history. History is itself a judgment.
The history of the world is also the court where all for-
malized institutions and styles must at last appear on trial,
as Hegel observed. We are judged by our own present laws
in so far as we profess membership in an institution, political or intellectual. But every secular institution also proposes its own perfection and so demands revision of
outlook. The motives that lead to natural knowledge, for
example, are not clear in their beginnings, and the essays
in fulfillment are subject to the forces that launched them.
It is, therefore, no part of the historical temper to say that
Parmenides was "right" in claiming that true being can
never change, and Heraclitus "wrong" in proposing perpetual flux. It is as barbarous to chip away at Plato as to
knock a bit of marble off the Parthenon. One may, and
one must, allege that the concerns that animated Plato
were not there brought to completion. But that is a judgment of history and not of an undefiled ahistoric omni-
science.

One does not stand on an Archimedean platform and
snipe at the universe or absolve oneself from time in order
to estimate the value of its disclosures. Nor can we suppose
that a depraved and stupid ancestry would recommend the
likelihood of our own virtue and genius. It is fair enough
to see shortcomings provided that by their means we see
greatness. "Until you understand a writer's ignorance,"
Coleridge remarks in *Biographia Literaria,* "consider yourself ignorant of his understanding." Every historical ignorance is also the locus of a historical understanding. Most
of us are capable only of standard errors, and we are then
forgiven, or instructed, or punished. But great men and
great times make mistakes and do deeds from which their
proper heirs recoil. But this means only that we are the
beneficiaries of great revisions, and not the emancipated

spectators of all time and all existence who need only to be careful and sober in order to be right.

This consideration seriously affects what one can think and say about the idea of history. It imposes a frame of mind to which we are unaccustomed but of which we have vague intimations when we feel that history is a mode of fatality. Goethe observes that what has been inherited must be reacquired if it is to be appropriated: *Was du geerbt von deinem Vater hast, erwirbt es um es zu besitzen.* If we possess the present we must make the pilgrimage that has so far advanced to this station. And if we may trust Emerson, we see in history the one mind that is "common to all individual men." But as a rule, we prefer to be right than to be in history. And that, in part, explains why so few of us enter by that narrow gate. Some men and some events make their time, but for the most part we only execute or imitate, and perhaps deface, the style which we have inherited.

It is easy to avoid judgment where one is not concerned. One has one's own affairs. But the avoidance of judgments upon morals and truth does not, in the historical temper, involve indifference. The moralizing and truth-telling person is not involved with the actual instance that he judges; he is identified only with the principle of the matter, and so with the abstract, not the actual. It is this aloofness to the actual that marks the ahistoric propensity. Since I know about logic, why should I not judge Aristotle; and since I possess the rules of morality, why should I not call the executioners of Joan of Arc wicked and savage men? Of course Shaw did not do that, and it is precisely this identification of himself with a fateful development rather than with any static code that has offended the orthodox, who know what's right and true. Our common sense knows only the indifferent, the censorious, or the practical.

History is the dimension in which we see ourselves, not as others see us, but as we are genetically identified. "There, but for the grace of God, go I" is not enough. One has to say, "There, by the abounding grace of God, I too find myself." There is great aversion even to a generous temper when it takes the form of fellow feeling rather than of a secure and tolerant superiority. Nobody can, by the grace of God, feel himself saved from participation in the enormities of the past, any more than he can dissociate his own heart and mind from its glories. But one has to take both or neither. One can't pick and choose, play Antonio but not Shylock, Portia but not Lady Macbeth. The disinterestedness of history is not of the same sort as that of the questioner of facts in some established frame of reference. In history we judge only that we may be judged; we aspire to be worthy of being overpassed, but not ignored.

Those who judge by conceiving themselves, at most, fallible in terms of present assurances are not in history. Tolerance has become an intellectual virtue too often associated with tentativeness, hesitation, and the fear that one may be mistaken. But Cromwell did not, in the end, establish the Commonwealth. The disinterestedness of history is resolute to declare the necessities of further development. It is as willful as the great acts that mark the moments of our enlarged energies. For it is these that have to be understood, and it is with these that one seeks identification. "What's Hecuba to him, or he to Hecuba, / That he should weep for her?" But Hamlet rather missed the point; the tears were not for Hecuba, they were rather an evidence of an emotional participation. One could weep for Hecuba and still be futile. William James speaks of the Russian lady who, on a bitter winter night, wept for the heroine at the opera while her coachman froze to death on the box waiting for her return. History is the place one goes when one gives up passing judgments and accepts identifications. It is the alternative to seeing all things *sub specie aeternitatis*. They are to be seen *sub specie temporis*. This is the heresy of history. But it is also the condition of all humanistic concerns.

A way out has been proposed. It is the way of the ecstatic moment that eludes judgment. The particular act made absolute—and each act is particular—loses the name of action. It loses limitation, answering to no specific situation and specific need, forgoing its claim to propriety and serviceability, which would reinstate the particular and the finite. The absolute moment has lost its momentum, coming from nowhere and going nowhere. It has lost its reason, and can make no claim to choice, direction, or resolution. It does not endure. It is not generative of time and consequences. It absorbs the agent so that he is lost in ecstasy or frenzy and is, as is said, "possessed." Nature or Dionysos or a demon inhabits him. How is one to reconcile Apollo, the god of light and articulate intelligence, with Dionysos, the patron and author of an ecstatic immediacy? Both are gods or, as we would say, principles and forces of human nature. Impulse encounters the malady of thought, and gray theory betrays the moment into a postponement of all absorption. So we want, at times, to take the cash, to seize the day and put a minimum of trust in a fickle tomorrow. *Dum loquimur fugerit invida aetas.* And "Had we but world enough, and time," we could ponder beauty itself as it deserves, but, alas, be deprived of its enjoyment.

15

The Simultaneous and the Successive

If one asks about the mode of identification of time there are many suggestions. But it seems clear that all of them depend on some inherent restlessness in an actual and specific moment. Time is recognized as such a moment moves into its own enlargement. It is the actuality of a moment, and a moment spreads both into the simultaneous and into the successive. The simultaneous is the moment of experience among its ideal contemporaries; the successive shows it in its genesis and its consequences. Intellect and theory occur in the simultaneous, resolution and will in the genetic. The simultaneous is also the locus of the practical; the sequential of the active risk and ultimate hazards. Without enlargement the moment contracts into an inarticulate stupidity and into a nerveless passivity. So it loses the name of thought and the name of action. But whether one's interests lie in the simultaneous that is nature or in the genetic that is history, there is no peculiar content of consciousness that occasions the expansion. Any content, so long as there is some content, will suit the emergence of the moment into the modes of time.

If one proposes to drive to New York—or to Boston, it doesn't matter which so long as it is one place or another—one goes by a map that, one hopes, shows the present roads and their condition. One has gas in the tank, because engines require fuel, and one sees to it that the apparatus and regularities of the vehicle have been duly taken into account. The purpose of driving to New York could be neither formulated nor executed apart from such a projection. These conditions of purpose are the simultaneous. They are nature. Here is the region of practice, of intellect and of theory. The simultaneous is the expansion of the moment into possibility of action and into possibility of theory. Here is the scientific and pragmatic, but not the historical, temper. In this context, all time is clock time, not historical time. It is the time of an ideal simultaneity, and consequently one can determine where one will be if one changes position in a given direction at forty miles per hour. This too is the region of facts, and not of acts, so much so that the very possibility of acts has been brought into question where time is interpreted as an ideal simultaneity within which changes occur.

Such changes express the variations of the unchanging and not the processes by which the present order has been developed and through which it is revised. This is the reason for the difficulties about the freedom of the will. There is no use looking for will among the facts. It is rather the energy which projects both the simultaneous and the passing. It is the moment maintaining its distinctness in its modes.

Historical time does not lie within the static and simultaneous, where one may come upon it tomorrow or the next day after diligent search. No actual present can be identified without antecedents that have precisely the feature of being undiscoverable in the contemporary. Time is no "pattern fixed in heaven," but rather the actuality of transition of a moment that only enlargement can identify. It is not the case that a moment passes; it is not something here today and gone tomorrow. Such views objectify time, as if the actual present took its place in a constancy independently identified. A past has the same actuality as the present of which it is the past, and every identifiable present requires its antecedents.

Events in nature succeed each other apropos of time, but

moments have no temporal framework within which they succeed each other. The moment has nowhere to go except into its own past and future or else into that simultaneity which defines its specific content. To say that one observes the passage of time as one would the waves on a beach is to abandon time as constitutional and immediate. Moments do not follow each other with a measurable frequency. They are not a class of entities, changing their colors, shapes, and position. The moment does not pass; rather, it has nowhere to go. It is only itself, and if it preserves itself it generates its sequel. Nor is it quite correct to speak of "successive" moments, as if moments were like cars in a train successively passing the observer at the station and ending with a caboose. Succession occurs apropos of time, but time does not pass apropos of time. Each car in the train could be cut out and left on a siding, but for time itself there are no such discrete moments and no station separate from moments from which one observes their passing. To allege that one observes the passing of time is to have abandoned it as a constitutional element, but in our tradition time has been the pensioner of eternity.

Any way of removing oneself from time discounts the actual. The humanities are at a disadvantage in the ideally simultaneous, whether this be spiritual or material. "Life, like a dome of many-colored glass, / Stains the white radiance of Eternity." "We look before and after, / And pine for what is not." The very word "ideal" has come to be associated with something out of time, and it is not clear whether "ideal" is an encomium or an epithet. The simultaneous may be regarded as ideal, but in itself it has no ideals. No doubt it was this difficulty that Plato faced in the *Symposium,* where love was declared to be no god, but a child of poverty and plenty, begotten in the abandonment of a revel where intoxication with the moment canceled the distinction between rags and riches.

Philosophy itself stands in the usual mind as an over-all view. One takes something "philosophically" when one sees the present in a larger setting. Then it is said that philosophy studies "the whole," or that it has "synoptic"

16

Memory and Morals

History gives rise to the idea of a present, where one means a very general state of affairs. "Memory" and "perception" are terms denoting past and present when no change in general outlook upon nature or self has occurred. For example, it is not quite accurate to say that one "remembers" one's youth, since its position and meaning depend upon recognizing what was not recognized when one was young. But if one "remembers" where one stored one's winter coat, one invokes the same world and outlook present when the coat was laid away. In general, there are two "presents," one for psychology and one for history. The nonpsychology "present" implies a nonpsychology "past." That there is a nonpsychology past is one way of saying that there is history.

A second point concerns the identification of history. This requires an actual and present sense of uncertainty about the general world in which one is living. Matter of fact contains no history and no past—nothing of thought, in short. The sense of the historical in the present is dependent upon very general uncertainty in thought and will. Perhaps it could be put, "What do I stand for?" This, of course, is not the same as "What do I want?" (for example, a brown hat or a gray one). History supposes the capacity to feel dissolution in the absence of an ability to stand for something.

That is much the same as feeling that one can't act at all

where one does not propose to influence the future. In the psychological present one does not propose to make one's deed correct beyond winning a subjective satisfaction. There is no question there of whether one shall act at all, or of giving shape to one's act, so as to make it the expression of a general outlook. Nor would one see that act as determining a general outlook. But in the apprehension of the idea of history the present uncertainty is the same as the need of exhibiting and endorsing a general outlook, one that has a future—one that has general consequences.

History links itself to morality in that way. It means the responsible act, the act that sustains a world, not just a subjective feeling of pleasure.

History appeals only to those who wish to make history. Morality is the first stage in the making of history because it joins act and its general meaning or destiny. If morality means more than pleasing oneself or others, and if it means something other than pleasing even God, it would seem that it means sustaining the will as absolute. This seems to have been an old insight: that impulse, or disorder, left one will-less or powerless. But, then, to what was the will to be directed? To direct the will toward itself is to give it no occasion or substance. That was Kant's shortcoming, at least in the accepted meaning of Kant.

But if the will must have occasion, then it must compound with the accidental. Still, the accidental as absolute has no form, and evokes no answer. The accidental occasion of will must itself have some authority. It has that because it is already part of "nature," part of an order. In fact, the power of the actual and accidental to evoke will is proportional to the meaning of some content for the sustaining of the order in which it occurs. The more "idealized" the occasion, the more compulsory it becomes for the will.

Those are interested in history who must idealize the occasion for action in order to have an occasion for action. Traditional morality seeks to idealize action without idealizing its occasion. That, in short, is the reason for the breakdown of ethics.

No occasion for action is "ideal" in the sense that it can evoke the perfect act, or the perfect satisfaction. But the occasion can get idealized in so far as it becomes the locus of further acts that create a region of will. There is no perfect college, or perfect town, or perfect man or woman. To "idealize the occasion" is only to seize upon it as a focus for expending the energies that sustain the world that produced the occasion. An occasion is seized upon for that promise. Action occurs as one has confidence in its occasions. This is more important than "self-confidence." Moralists try to give one confidence in such occasions by saying that one will win happiness, do good, or please God.

History occurs in the breakdown of morality. A very moral person would not, I think, get to the idea of history, because the occasion for action would always be clear to him. And, of course, the makers of history are often viewed as immoral because they cannot abide the moral occasions of action. They can't act morally—that is, in terms of mores. But they propose to act, and in that way differ from the immoralist.

The sense of history seems to occur only with the systematic collapse of morals. That is where we stand. I do not think that the Greeks or Romans ever contemplated such a condition. The Church saw that morals had in fact broken down, and it restored them by making the occasion for action an opportunity for transcendental idealization. To this day the Church insists that there is no other mode of idealization of the occasion for action.

The true record for the appearance of the idea of history is formed among the moralists. Science is contributory, but oblique. History appears when the occasion for action is seen to be intrinsically ideal. But that result is originally obscured since action first appears in the service of purposes or of God.

Our lack of confidence is, from this point of view, a historical phenomenon. But it has the curious quality of running along with unprecedented effort and energy. Somehow, the ideal is already in the occasion for action.

This is the converse of Kant. Any occasion for action has merit. It is better than doing nothing. We dislike boredom and to avoid it we will do a jig if necessary. This does not mean that we have no resources. It means that the traditional resources end by clouding action itself. That is what we won't have. But this seems to me no mere decay, but rather an evidence that morality for us means doing something no matter what. Solitude and inaction are to be avoided. We like busy and active people.

So the uneasiness that prompts history is a radical uneasiness. It is based on misgivings over the secular, and also over the transcendent. This seems to be the impasse in which it appears. I think it is a phase of the impasse between skepticism and dogmatism, which itself is felt only as the blockage of energy and not as an impersonal fact or theory. The conflict of those two positions occurs only as the restlessness of an attitude that is both self-seeking and disciplined. As the record of freedom, history is also the idea of self-discipline. Since it is a radical idea, it must occur as an answer to radical, not speculative, conflict,—that is, as conflict of attitudes understood as volitional and passionate. Skepticism and dogmatism seem to be the radical attitudes that give rise to the sense of history.

This seems to me a more promising way of putting the case than the question about controls of act, the question of fate. The question about fate seems to be, Does the world allow for my will, and if so, how? The question in terms of actual conflict is, Does my will allow for a world, and how? Both dogmatism and skepticism are consequences of a search for the authority of will and thought, or, in general, of personality.

17

Memory and the Humanities

No one lives in a world identical with that of his forefathers. The price of identifying one's present world is the perception of its contrast with an earlier view of man and nature. The New Testament succeeded the Old, as the Old succeeded a less definite status for Abraham before his call. We are conscious of the present only through its differences from a previous condition from which we have emerged, which we now repudiate but do not disavow as the ancestor of our present self-identity. No recognized outlook is quite amorphous; rather, each bears the mark of some transition in terms of which it enjoys or laments its later phase. Accounts of scientific method celebrate the emancipation of thought from the bondage of theology, metaphysics, or downright ignorance, and this contrast allows the advocate of science to identify himself, his outlook, and his epoch. The American Civil War marked a "new birth of freedom," a new outlook on the meaning of citizenship.

This dimension of change in time defines the studies called the humanities. Face to face with objects alone we are conscious but not self-conscious. To be self-conscious is to pay attention to one's own past, to one's deeds and thoughts, and especially to one's errors. No one can declare that he is guided by experience until he identifies the dimension of time. For this reason the religions of mankind have been a chief locus of the cult of personality.

We *have done* the things we ought not to have done and in the past tense discover a present selfhood. No logical problem, and no moral problem, can occur apart from this confrontation of the present by a deed that once was also present. In a novel or play, plot is the consequence of a deed, the launching into one's world of consequences that are visited upon the agent, to his undoing in tragedy, to his eventual correction and recovery in comedy. Even very poor novels, poems, or plays are likely to contain some ingredient of revelation, some reflection upon feeling, some appraisal of past excitement, or even the devised extension of a mood however silly or maudlin.

The past that appears to the humanist is not exhausted in memory, but involves always this process of redefinition of the person and his world. Memory is a psychological, not a historical concept. It is a formal ingredient in the recognition of an object, without which no object can attain outline or clarity. An object is now what one has found it out to be. We do not merely "find" objects, we "find them out" and so discriminate among them, and in this process of discrimination the object attains its definition and meaning. But the focus of attention in the learning process is the object itself, not one's reasoning processes or even one's psychological operations. As soon as we look at the propriety of a statement, we are no longer dealing with objects but with our own thought processes, and so we study logic, a discipline notably neutral to particular information. We may also study psychology, a science not designed to tell us how many planets of the sun there may be in the sky, or how much the dollar of the day can buy in terms of the celebrated and lamented dollar of years past.

What one remembers finds its primary evidence in what one can now say or do about a particular object as a result of having encountered it before, observing it, handling it, comparing it, and in all ways testing it to find out what it is in relation to other objects. But such procedures do not include the humanities or the historical past. They show how one changes opinions about particular things, but not.

how one changes one's general orientation. That cannot be done by a closer discrimination of particular objects. Children pick up much information of this simple sort and may show surprising knowledge of autos, baseball records, the place to look for frogs, the hermit thrush, or the lady's-slipper. This elementary and ever-charming wonder so refreshing and sometimes saddening to adults precedes the more troubled arrival of formal problems, whether about nature or human nature. It is the age of innocence, where, surely, history has no place. Nor do any other of the humanistic concerns appear until time abolishes the fresh spontaneities of a varied but untroubled engagement with a serene and vivid present.

18

The Past as an Influence

The idea of history rests on the simple and generally held belief that the past continues to be influential in the present, and that both past and present carry intimations of their own future. That the past is a force, even though not found in nature but only in experience, is a crucial consideration in the establishment of history as a dimension of knowledge. This may seem a needless emphasis. But there is reason to believe that our traditional views of events do not contemplate a past that plays a role in the present and in the future. And yet, it is precisely such influence that alone could give the past a status as real. We call real only that which is influential. We look for the causes of events, for those controls of which appearances are the products and consequences. It is a good general rule that the real is the efficacious. The real is not the different, but what makes a difference.

Persons avoid the ineffectual, and if one does no more than plant a tree or speak a kind word, one has left a mark. Slavery is a condition in which persons do not count; that is its evil. Charms and magic do not cure diseases or change the weather; that is their unreality.

In all its historical nomenclature—God, nature, atoms, reason, personality—the real is always a force, a control, a determiner. The question of the status and meaning of history turns on the acknowledgment of influences that dwell only in time. This is the heresy of history; it is the reason why it is baffling or even repugnant.

Everyone knows the celebrated statement of Leopold von Ranke that the aim of the historian is to tell about events as they "really happened." It appears, however, that nobody has ever denied that aim. Nobody thinks that history starts out to be fiction. Aristotle preferred poetry to history as a vehicle of understanding because in poetry one attained a general view about man and his acts, whereas history seemed to him episodic and incapable of order. To discover what "really happens" is no doubt an excellent rule to apply to all knowledge, but we always approach the decision as to what really happened in terms of some test. One does not come to the real in relaxed passivity. One sets it apart from the unreal and the illusory. These tests become the precise locus of philosophic conflict. One could hardly, for example, claim that what really happened can be determined by the test of a present sensation or perception. We no longer hear the words of Pericles or Paul; there is no telecast of Marathon or the Constitutional Convention of 1787. All our yesterdays have vanished from the immediacy of our present. In this way the past, although once experienced, becomes as much a matter of thought as the last atom and the perceptual nullity of zero.

Knowledge, we often suppose, grows from psychology. But, apart from behaviorism, in which all subjectivity is denied, psychology assumes the data of sense and the interpretations of perception. Memory is someone's. There is no memory in general, and one must go to a person for reminiscence. But the historical past is not formed in memory. The past is not the experience of any one man, nor yet of all men put together in some vast incoherence without selection—aimless, amorphous. The dreams, illusions, or tumult of innumerable persons, their hopes, fears, and delights, fail to make a force of the past.

19

Memory as Control

The most elementary mode of the influence of the past is in memory. What one does today takes yesterday's experience into account. Once bitten, twice shy. Such memory and learning occur apropos of purposes, of limited aims and specific situations. In this context all experience is psychological. It is what it happens to be, and implies no antecedent necessity in the data that the execution of a purpose encounters. Where a purpose is itself taken to be accident, all that it encounters is no less so. The reason why a radical empiricism of this sort leaves data without necessity is that no purpose is itself viewed as a necessity. It is only an urge, a desire, a propensity, a tendency. Where, so to say, one "finds" oneself hungry or afraid, curious or indifferent, attracted or repelled, one also finds that the experiences that mark the actual extension of such ungoverned impulses are no less ungoverned. An earlier psychology, before the advent of instinct theory and the biological point of view, lacked even the directional control of purpose. The classic concept is the ancient one of the wax tablet, the completely clear and neutral receptacle of impressions. A chief modern instance occurs in David Hume, where one encounters the denial of all necessary connections, so that belief and action express the quite accidental association of ideas and nothing more. This point of view has been of very great influence and is still entertained by those who mistrust any systematic controls. We do what we happen to do; we believe what we happen to learn. Any impulse may vanish; any sequence of experience may vary as unaccountably as it has, for a time, remained constant. All rules are off, and anything is possible—if, indeed, the idea of possibility can be established on such premises.

On these terms, one is not well equipped to deal with controls and influences, with forces or restraints. There should be no easy disregard of the powerful currents of sober thought that have been suspicious of the whole idea of influences.

Force is not itself a datum. Wherever one meets with the idea of control, one has gone beyond appearances into a reality that does not itself appear. If one says that the past is "influential," that it is a force or determinant, one has cast some organizing unity over things as they merely happen. Memory makes optimists of us all. It engenders expectations and so permits confusions when our expectations fail. Memory leads to definition and so to exclusion and so to order. Stones are not good for building a fire, nor sticks for building a fireplace. Purpose, when specific, can operate only on the specific, and so there looms the limited object that has a "nature," and therefore implies that it is not some other object. Experience breaks out into order as soon as it entails identification and negations. Radical empiricism abolishes control because negation has no content. It is a thing of form. It is an ideal, not an impression or a datum. There is no quality that is a negation or restriction and no sense organ for discovering that a stick is not a stone.

To say, then, that the past is influential because memory is influential may be somewhat glib and superficial. Our yesterdays have no power in the present where experience has no career. Experience has a career only because it is not passive, but critical. And if critical, then even at the level of purpose, it involves rejections and therefore an order that is the vehicle of its force.

20

Prediction

People have always predicted. Medicine men knew how to bring things to pass, and therein lay their power. There may have been some risk in this, but so is there in any prediction. The priests of Baal lost to the priests of Jehovah; the event demonstrated the true belief, and was intended to. Wherever found, prediction has the important feature of relating order to the particular. Eleaticism rejected the coincidence of knowing with particular events. The predictive view insists on this coincidence. The constancies of nature are not abandoned, but they have acquired a close relation with the local, the psychological, and the actual. The universal is no longer the absolute reason itself. It is a regularity that we now defend as the way of saving actual particulars. The impersonal and anonymous order of nature has made alliance with the specific occasions of discovery.

The prestige of natural science has come to be derived no less from this relevance of the actual than from the impersonality of its results. Nature has moved into the dimension of control. Where there is control, there is a local authority. Banish that, and prediction reverts to psychological association where no limits can be imposed on accidental perceptions, and where any alleged limit reflects only some accident of a passive consciousness. But a prediction is more than a shot in the dark; the local has gained authority. In actuality it would seem rather more odd to propose that prediction has no place in experience than to claim that it does. The rational world must then make room for its occasion. We move toward the historical dimension. We invoke the here and now in order to support the order of nature itself.

One predicts no event in saying that the area of a right triangle will be half the area of the rectangle formed by its sides. Prediction of events occurs where the event includes an object that already has status in a *general* order—place, size, shape, quality, generic classification, or the like. But this object permits prediction because it is also a *particular* object—salt, aspirin, wood, an animal.

Such prediction is not, however, just permitted; it is *required*. Any common noun entails consequences.

There is no state of affairs not already involving prediction about which prediction is *subsequently* made.

He who can predict is said to know the ways of things; but he cannot predict until the things he knows already have *some* predictable ways. The root of prediction is identification. Say "water" and you have made a prediction. Also, unless you say "water" or "horse," no prediction is made.

All identification is also action. What one expects of water or a stone is a matter not of observation but of doing. There is no such object in terms of passivity alone. Passivity has notoriously lost the object—that is, the status of object. This status is acquired in the functional, not the perceptual, context. Water or any other object is known only as it is continuous with functioning—with drinking, say, or building a fire. Except in the service of function, perception is only the stream of consciousness, where no object is perceived.

The limits of objects occur in function. The negative—"water is *not* wood"—occurs in activity, not in a passive perception. Prediction requires this statement: "If I *do* so-and-so, then I will perceive so-and-so." Or, "Because so-and-so is done, so-and-so will ensue."

Passivity, in contrast, has no consequences because it has

no premise. It lacks any object about which a prediction follows. We must be rid of the view that prediction follows on observation, but not observation on prediction. Passivity does not observe. It has no focus or limits. In passivity there are no directions.

Prediction antedates natural science. The Fates spin, measure, cut. The balance of Zeus predetermines the victor in a battle. The stars in their courses fight against Sisera. Prediction is a determinism.

Any prediction falls within an assumed control. If I had no control over water, I could have no expectations about it. This control grows more refined when I can break up water into two gases or compose it from gases. Molecules and atoms appear as factors of control, particularly of quantitative control, as two volumes of hydrogen to one of oxygen. The locus of control is function, in this case measuring, a present active participle.

In the predictive view of knowledge the appearance "verifies" the anticipations of a present subjectivity. There we need to be forever anxious to win the incessant approval of an alien authority, so that knowledge-seeking can have the flavor of status-seeking on the part of the personally insecure. One may doubt that the social phenomenon of looking for status could have acquired so much momentum had there not been a more general insecurity fostered by a view of nature that saw it as the gleanings of a mistrusted subjectivity. And if, in order to avoid such a result, one falls back on some authority in the functioning person, then one has introduced action as a complement to the facts.

We predict reaction. We don't rub someone the wrong way, or speak of rope in the house of a man who has been hanged. But so soon as we predict an act, rather than an event in an object, we also face the uncertainty of a modification of controls. This uncertainty is the price of alleging the act. A man "comes to see" that tariffs do not necessarily protect jobs, he not having sufficiently understood the implications of his original premise. So one may find it unnecessary to keep still about the desirability of international trade.

One can predict an event within a static order; one cannot predict the changes of any such order. Euclid did not predict the rejection of the parallel postulate.

The nonpredictable is the historical. Yet all prediction occurs within a static view that is itself historical. Action is in principle unpredictable because it generates the relatively static orders within which all prediction occurs.

To contrive to make a person predictable in behavior is to destroy that other person. To treat others and all else as predictable is to destroy oneself as a person.

Thus the predictable falls within the unpredictable. The converse—that the unpredictable falls within the predictable—leaves the predictable without authority or hold on the alleged person who asserts it. For that hold is his actual control, in his functioning.

The unpredictable is not the vagrant. Historical changes are likely to appear so to the static outlook. Science itself was once opposed; yet it is a consequence of the activities of its enemies, even as they defined terms or weighed a pound of bread or set measured limits to their acres. Grammar and logic are controls, but so is dialectic, of which the shape was not fully noted. In terms of logic there was no philosophy and no history, but in terms of psychology there is no logic. The relations are dialectical.

The questions about the predictable are all dialectical—that is, structural and ontological. To say, as above, that prediction is not subsequent to perceptions of objects but is required in the identification of objects is to make prediction constitutional and essential, not something that supervenes or is the peculiar power of the scientist.

Prediction requires formality, but form is not predictable within a static control. Form is actual, not perceptual. This goes even for arithmetic. Control emerges from prior controls, incomplete, but not quite chaotic. *Ex post facto* we are not surprised at the collapse of the ancient *polis*. It could not control the purposes that had recommended it. The Roman Empire displaced Aristotle. Nor was that empire nothing but a brutal conquest. Rome, itself originally a *polis,* did what was necessary for its own power. If Greece took captive its conqueror, it was not the Greece of Plato's or Aristotle's *polis*. That Greece could captivate Rome shows that the *polis* was more than a restricted power.

People feel on solid ground when they can predict. And so they are. But that ground is not itself predictable. The force of the prediction derives from the activity in which it is inherent. If I can do *anything,* I can predict. But a prediction is not an action subsequent to passivity. Any act entails a prediction and vice versa.

21

Documentation

A discussion of history does well to avoid an alienation from natural science so abrupt that in the end the two interests will confront each other as incommunicable. At the same time one can hardly avoid differences that at first do seem alienating. Science eventuates in formulae, and while such universalities bring release from a broken and disorderly privacy where the self is blurred in confusion and impotence, they omit all reference to things done. History, in contrast, needs acts, agents, dates, places, desires, and passions. In order to study these it employs a peculiar sort of material—namely, documents and monuments. These are the residues of acts, not objects of nature. Can one allege "knowledge" on the basis of such materials? Obviously not, if by knowledge one means one's relation with precisely that region from which acts are excluded. Nature contains no libraries or museums, does not produce them, does not cherish them, and may destroy them. The document, furthermore, speaks of a local event; it may be even what someone thought about nature, but as a historical document it is only the disclosure of a view peculiar to its time and place, and it may not, in its content, in what it says, be received as an acceptable account of the very objective world in which the historian himself is standing.

There appears, then, a difference in style between physics and history, and this can be troublesome because of the great authority enjoyed by the study of nature. A question in history always sends one to a document for an answer, to a monument of some sort. We go there for an answer because it was apropos of some dated event that the question about the past was raised. The American Revolution has complex antecedents, including taxes imposed to help defray the costs of the French and Indian War, the authority of Parliament, the temper and character of the colonists. What is said in these ways about the Revolution needs "documentation" in a quite literal sense. Documents are not objects of nature. They are all artifacts, residues of acts, part of an act left over, often deliberately made and no less deliberately preserved.

As an item in nature the Rosetta stone may suggest the process of rock formation, but in that capacity it says nothing about Egyptians and Greeks and discloses no equivalence of linguistic symbols. If one wanted to know the weight of the Rosetta stone it would be convenient to find a note about it in the encyclopedia, but lacking that, one could always answer the question by putting the stone on scales. That question is not about the past, nor does the answer tell about the events and deeds of yesterday. Gravitation is dateless, no more a phenomenon of the ancient world than of our own. It is said of Thales of Miletus that he predicted the eclipse of May 28, 585 B.C. That an eclipse did occur has been asserted by astronomers, but no planetarium informs us that a man named Thales existed and exhibited an interest in astronomy. We could know that the eclipse took place quite apart from any documents mentioning Thales, but in the absence of documents we are unable to say what was being done or studied in sixth-century Caria.

The style of history, the structure of its statements, could hardly avoid being influenced by these documented occasions any more than the style of physics can avoid expressing an irrelevance to the dated artifact. Style is not only the man; it is also the mode of expression of a distinctive subject matter. Nature does not preserve artifacts, and it may destroy them, but we do preserve them, deliberately and at some expense. What they say cannot be reproduced in the present tense. Time requires its appropriate medium, the distinctive objects that reveal it, objectify it, and are its substance. In history there is no temporally neutral region awaiting our inspection at such times as may be convenient to our practical purposes or theoretical interests. We find, rather, a curious requirement that we participate in the past if it is to be available. People say of nature, "It is there all the time," intending by this to convey nature's independence of our notice, or even of our existence. Dubious as such an idea may be, it is uttered with an evident expectation that there will be no objection to it. But the past is not there "all the time," at least not any past open to historical study. It depends on our attending to it. What is there "all the time" has nothing historical about it.

Historical narrative appears early in Western literature, but the "idea" of history found positive expression more recently, first with Vico and then at fuller length with Hegel. To say that history became an idea is to propose that it appeared as a constitutional factor of experience, so that every mode of discourse, and every statement, exhibits a historical aspect. A large dictionary tells what a word "means" by giving its "derivation" and by supplying an account of past usages that mark its career. To a lawyer the law is what it has become, and this specification of the actual occasions when a rule has been applied and qualified, far from detracting from the force of law, adds, rather, to its weight and authority.

History appeared as idea when it was discovered that we stood in experience. It is not so much that we prized experience, as if it were a good thing, and quite helpful, and much better than snap judgment. It is rather to say that no present truth or action could be understood without an appeal to time, and to past time. We are now what we have come to be, and apart from that transformation we do not know ourselves.

Ortega concludes a section in *History as a System* on this note. The past, if it is to be found at all, must be in the present. "The past is not yonder, at the date when it happened, but here, in me. The past is I—by which I mean my life." One way of coming to understand what he means is suggested by asking what there is about the present that serves as a vehicle of the past. What brings a past to notice, and why should it seem important, could we find it? An attic is likely to harbor mementos, children's toys, an old chest, perhaps letters or bills. As a rule one's attachment to such items is utilitarian or sentimental. They have no lasting value. It might even facilitate housekeeping to be rid of them. But should there be found a first edition of *Uncle Tom's Cabin,* the local historical society might be interested. In fact, there are many fine buildings that exist in order to house and to guard books, documents, paintings, and scientific apparatus. We are glad when through benefactors these are acquired by a public institution. Then, too, there is a widespread interest in genealogy even though some scion—in a collateral line—stood with the royalists.

We can believe without much strain that the present would be the poorer without these mementos, which bring us participation in yesterday. To make a sharper point: it is as if the life of the present would lose much of its vigor and tenacity if it were to be deprived of its continuity with those who have gone before, finding no evidence of their presence, and so without heritage.

In *The Ancient City,* Fustel de Coulanges centers the sense of personal identity, as it was felt by Greeks and Romans, on ancestral piety. The dead still belonged to the family, and the family to them. They guarded the living members and received daily homage. Not to share in such a tradition was to be an outcast or a slave. These practices went beyond private sentiment. They had, indeed, nothing to do with the separated person but only with those whose individuality grew from, and depended on, a community stretching into the past. This membership was the locus of obligations. It defined rights and duties, friends and enemies. It summoned virtue and exertion. It led to *res gestae.* It supported a view of the nature of men and gods.

The celebrated "contract" theory of society treats the individual as if he could decide by himself whether or not to join the commonwealth. No doubt this view has importance in so far as it accentuates the question of the basis of our relation to society, and if one is to give an answer in historical terms, the contract theory does a good job. Today we speak of getting "adjusted" to society, as if that were the problem. And, of course, we then have the rather neglected, and complementary, difficulty of discovering how society is to adjust to us. For the complete egoist this has no answer short of the subjugation of society to his own purpose.

The past seems to lie about us. But there may be conveyed by such examples an illusory sense of accidental discovery, as if one stumbled upon the past as upon a sea shell at a beach. The case is rather that where nothing is cherished nothing is found. Now this seems to be a matter of some weight, but likely to be passed over, or denied, in our factually oriented idiom. For to cherish requires emotion and will. If there are to be memorials, they have to be treated as memorials. There are no monuments of the past as matters of fact, or as phenomenal appearances, or as scientific data. There are no monuments in terms of the traditional epistemology of passivity. A past has to be actively treasured if it is to be perceived as a past. This leads at once to the factor of voluntarism in history. Ortega and many others point out that history deals with things done, *res gestae,* and so it does. But while there is no history where nothing has been done, and while there is no "reality"—shall we say—apart from the past tense, still neither is there any history where the present tense is not itself defined through the will. And this present willfulness exhibits the historical dimension only as it deliberately cherishes its antecedents as a condition of its own articulate force. The past is not casually discovered as an area of "acts" rather than of facts. It is only a present willfulness that has any interest in the past, and then only when, without its past, it would lose its *raison d'être.* The historical is not, then, intellectually descried. One does not stumble upon it as another interesting oddity in an assumed present. There is no present unless it gets known, and it is not known until it finds its meaning in its antecedents. It takes time to know a present. This is one of the basic aspects of the idea of history.

Yet mathematics and logic, which have a purely formal ingredient, are often regarded as the very patterns and models of responsible statement. Combined in some way—a rather mysterious way—with psychology, they are taken to box the compass of human knowledge. Sense data, clothed in mathematics and logic, have, in fact, been represented as the proper figure of a knowledgeable man. Any other vesture is but the rags and tatters of a vagrant fancy and even of a delusive nonsense. But in mathematics and logic one looks in vain for our yesterdays, for dusty death or a jubilant tomorrow. No theorem establishes an actuality. None refers to an object, or to a subject. None concerns the unquiet that seeks relief in any specific act. Content is an irrelevance. Indeed, ever since Pythagoras and his admirer Plato, pure form has had a tendency to remove itself from content, leaving us with questions about the relation of these two factors of ordinary experience. No question in philosophy has had a longer run. Content, the accidental, has seemed not necessary either in detail or as an ontological constituent of the verb "to be"; form, the universal, has seemed most authoritative as it acknowledged neither genesis nor sequel in a troubled and incomplete finitude. For such an admission would, it is thought, invalidate the claim of form to a critical precedence, to that control over all that we happen to know without which we would wander in unregulated opinion or sentiment.

If it is the psychologist who names the springs of action, the drives, urges, hungers, instincts, aversions, and appetites, and if he is the one who traces out the process of their execution, and if all that is done is a manifestation of such forces, then the historian has nothing essentially new to disclose about man. And if it is one's object to study "human nature," why not turn to anthropology, to the laboratories of the psychologist, to statistical records of "behavior," in order to learn what controls the peculiar phenomenon called action? Perhaps, too, history should be turned over to the psychiatrists, who make a point of inquiring into those qualities of action associated with narrowly concentrated energies, particularly when it is alleged that they aim at some desperate expression of the ego, some excited attempt at public notice, some hope of remaking the world nearer to the heart's desire, some crusading utopian dream.

Is there anything more to Caesar's *Gallic Wars* than a psychological disclosure? Artists of all sorts have also been made the objects of a scientific analysis, while the characters of novels and plays serve as examples of a psychological maladaptation. On such premises the literary historian had best study Freud, and then he will be able to show how Oedipus, Hamlet, Faust, and Ahab can serve as admirable illustrations of quite ahistoric features of human nature, illustrations of dark forces lurking in any man and quite as dateless as the relations of temperature, pressure, and volume in Boyle's law.

It is true that most ways of talking psychology employ the idea of "memory" openly or covertly and so suggest a past. Still, no one now alive remembers the Etruscans or the landing at Plymouth Rock. Memory is one's own, and nobody remembers another's life or experience. Not only that; one may be at a loss to understand how anyone ever thought of building the Parthenon or Amiens, and it could be dangerous to assume that one could tell in terms of a twentieth-century outlook. The historical past can be puzzling; so can one's own. No act manifests a total control of the forces that produced it—a consideration that haunts totalitarian managers and worries perfectionists. What one was like at the age of ten one did not then know and so cannot now remember. At thirty, one may perhaps have made a few sketches, to one's amusement or alarm. We may come trailing clouds of glory later darkened by the shades of a mundane prison house, but it seems rather more likely that we appeared incoherent and impish to others and, after a time, to ourselves as well. "Just like his father," people say, and even father may find the disclosure both novel and embarrassing. Memory has limits. But in both history and biography we face not the limits of memory but its formal incompetence.

In reading a history book one sometimes receives the impression that the historian fancies himself to have been present at a transaction and that he is telling what he, as an acute observer, would have been able to report had he been alive at that earlier time. Inasmuch as he was not there and so cannot claim to have perceived and now to remember the event, he does the next-best thing and consults the records. The records may be somewhat incomplete, vague, or even contradictory, but so are reports of contemporary events—say, a traffic accident or a supposed German raid on Halifax during the First World War. So one has to sift the reports and use one's judgment. In view of the distinctive role played by documents in history, this reliance on report is essential.

But does it follow that one thereupon tells the story as if one had been there, that one could do so, or that one would want to; or that if one could do so and wanted to do so, one would be writing history? A twentieth-century person brought up on William James, John Dewey, and a dash of Wittgenstein might not understand what was going on at Agathon's party in the *Symposium*. There is a story about Mark Twain which tells that he practiced profanity with copious eloquence, to the distress of his wife. Other remedies having failed, it occurred to her that if she learned the techniques of his deplorable habit and confronted him with his own verbiage, he would be shocked into reform. After careful study she did one day speak to him in his own idiom. Very much astonished, he looked at her for a moment and said, "My dear, you have the words but not the music." To hear the music of the *Symposium* one might very well need to absent oneself somewhat from the felicities of the present, causing one's contemporaries to entertain doubts of one's sound practical orientation when one should be making ready to assume "leadership" in the troubled and demanding present. The present tense of any one person does not include the historical past as either an actual or a possible memory. Indeed, the past looms only in so far as the present is threatened with some disqualification, so that to understand itself as present it needs to undertake a story of its genesis. Sometimes the contemporary disposes of the past as showing only oddity, ignorance, or error from the point of view of the present outlook; sometimes the present itself is viewed askance when some past way of life or belief has not been preserved by a misled or degenerate posterity.

What one is to do about any document, or how one is to understand it, is not determined by a psychological stimulus, by its color, shape, or taste, or by any static property that marks it as one natural object rather than another. In so far as the account of "perception" describes the consciousness of any object to which one responds purposefully, it fails to include the artifactual, the symbolic, in their peculiar historical status. Animals and barbarians may have sharp senses and have learned how to enact their impulses, but the symbol, and so the past, has no meaning to them. There are, to be sure, artifacts that induce a characteristic response—a bell, a cry, a light, an object—but such data operate only as signals, producing a standard reaction as if they were part of the purpose-world, part of the "real" world, whether natural or supernatural, to which one has become "adapted" by making the proper response. In those studies called "liberal arts" no specific techniques directed toward a determinate end can be inculcated. The psychology of learning fails in the apprehension of the unique, the individual, the dated, the past, the vocal or eloquent symbol.

22

The "Referent" of a
Statement in History

Do statements in history have denotation, and if so, what might the referent be?

It seems clear that no such referent is observable. One can't observe Columbus discovering America. All the past, including the last moment, eludes any sensory apprehension or perception. Most of the past is not even "remembered"—that is, it is no part of the memory of any living person. One can't invoke that good old standby, so much abused, of "pointing" to a past event. It is nowhere under the sun.

This would be an exasperating result were the past event analogous to an object that had once been open to perception, but had now faded from view. But while there can be no present perception of a past event, this need not lead us to suppose some baffling defeat in historical statements. There never is a historical event as historical, until it is past, and apprehended as past. Were all events capable of present perception there would be no history.

Nor would there be a history could one simply report on what happened. No report of what happens is knowledge. Knowledge requires some mode of viewing or arranging the events that happen. Report contains no basis for making any demands on the data. One cannot cross-examine them. They do not answer one's questions. To give one's questions a status is to assume some authority over the materials regarding their truth and their importance. One wants them to satisfy one's criteria of truth and of importance.

The past, moreover, cannot be approached all at once, as if from some position not affected by it. The transition to the past is not external. The past appears in the present.

Indeed, to have a present at all is to have some meaning for the past. That meaning occurs in some object which the present does not explain. That object is some sort of residue left by a past act, a document of some sort, perhaps written, perhaps merely an artifact. But history is an interest in the past for its own sake. The historical document deliberately records the past. It is not an accidental remainder. When dealing with the past for its own sake one does so apropos of something specific in the present. One does not look to the past as a whole, but to the past apropos of a concrete state of affairs.

There is no history of the past, but there is a history of the Peloponnesian War. That war becomes historical because it is somehow worthy of being recorded. To neglect it is to be vague about the present. For one observes that the present is peculiar. The past permits us to understand that present, that specific and peculiar present. Accordingly, what happened in the past is determined by the present interest. Nor can one say that the event happened in the past except from the standpoint of a present question. The past is no more out of reach than is the present.

Consequently there is the view that history can gain no objectivity, every history being written from the point of view of one's own time, its values and beliefs. Thus the story of the past changes.

True, all history does express a particular time, place, and culture. The past reflects the present. But what is there in this present that colors the past? It is not what is subjective in the present. The subjective has no past but is mere appearance or seeming, or thought. The order of appearance is psychology, the career of one's own experience.

Within those limits no question of veracity or fidelity to truth can occur. Psychology tells how it comes about that one feels, thinks, or acts as one does. It does not, however, give an account of whether one thinks truly, or feels sensibly, or acts efficiently or wisely. Psychology can propose no past that could have any properties or career apart from some one person's seeming or experience.

Yet history aims to tell how events occurred, what governed their occurrence as events, not as someone's thoughts or beliefs, but as objective, as common to many persons, as something that happened apart from anyone's believing it happened. History constrains belief; it can correct belief. It is not a region of unchecked fancy. Science also constrains belief; opinions secure confirmation or rejection in view of another factor, the nonpsychological order of events. Their order, as shared by all, is available to all. So one commonly assumes.

Yet this is more than an assumption. It is rather the condition of discovering and labeling the subjective. Thus any science offers a foil to opinion. When one says that a belief is only an opinion, one can give specific meaning to this statement only by exhibiting some difference between opinion and something not subjective. This is the price to pay for the use of the word "subjective." There is need for something more than psychology in order to disclose thought as having a personal factor. Were all experience psychological and nothing more, no contrast between appearances and facts would be proposed.

History concerns that factor of experience which constrains belief. At any present moment there occur both belief and what constrains it—that is, both the psychological and the objective or the impersonal or the common. This factor is the present account of the form of this objective and constraining element. History deals with the career of the distinction between the psychological and the objective. Thus our present world is causal rather than purposive; it is naturalistic rather than theistic; it is individualistic rather than dogmatic; it is spatially and temporally coherent rather than separate; it is pragmatic rather than

contemplative; intellectual rather than mystical; psychological rather than logical; skeptical rather than naïve. All
these distinctions register some view of the way things
really are, within which the subjective factor occurs. Thus
all events have a mathematical side, or a causal side. These
properties of events are the modes of sifting out the true
picture from the merely subjective one. More and more
refinement of the modes of distinguishing between appearance and fact has occurred. The career of this refinement is
history.

Thus history is the story not of appearances, but of the
differences by which appearances have been set off from
reality. History begins with some present account of the
shape and properties of the nonsubjective, and traces its
genesis and growth.

This is, to be sure, a growth of thought. But it is also
the growth of that factor of thought which permits the
distinction between appearance and reality. It is the growth
of the nonsubjective factor of thought.

Thus history is the revelation of law, for it is law that
sets off opinion from truth. We have today more types of
law than used to be the case, more illustrations of how
opinion can be policed by the impersonal structure of
thought. Thus physics is the consequence of the discovery
of the distinction between opinion and knowledge with
regard to nature; political philosophy, or government, the
discovery of the difference between desire and the laws
that govern desires. Thus we can now say of the criminal
that he neglects the law of his own will, whereas in quite
early times the difference between one man and another
was rather one of desires than of desire versus law. The
education of a man or of a society lies in this discovery of
the modes of discipline.

Hence freedom equals objectivity.

Also, the story of objectivity or of freedom is not subjective.

History is written apropos of an absolute distinction of
subjectivity from objectivity. We find ourselves in history.
About "finding" there is an interesting ambiguity; on the

one side, the found seems less authoritative than the profound, as when a statement of fact appears as an inference,
or a sum as the result of a process of addition. As we say,
we "check" it. On the other side, what is found is often
regarded as peculiarly insistent, a presence requiring that it
be taken into account, as when one finds that one has an
unexpected dollar in one's winter-coat pocket or that on
Candlemas Day one should still have half one's oats and
half one's hay. One may find that people who justify
themselves by an appeal to "conscience" leave one peculiarly helpless and not knowing why one feels exasperated
and frustrated rather than pleased with so lofty a defense.

One finds errors, but not until one has made some. If
one then looks to discover how errors get made, one
encounters operations of some sort. In the case of fallacies
one encounters logic. What one has already been saying
begins to take on shape and order. The discovery that we
live in a logical world can burst upon one with the same
effect of emancipation as many have felt when, on no better authority than their own, they proved a proposition in
geometry. To say of a person that he lacks logical sense
carries a different flavor from saying that he has not visited
Outer Mongolia. The deficiency is a comment on his self-
control and so on his self-consciousness, as if he were not
holding himself together in his words, not using them as
a base for further and entailed statements launched by what
he had said. The disclosure of a logical immediacy is the
presence of form in what had seemed vagrantly accidental.
Its force as a disclosure is the same as its identity with the
speaker.

On the other side, neither is there a psychological
account of the historical person and his world. Both psychology and logic deal with the accidental and that is why
both are confronted in the end with a begged question, the
psychologist with the whole apparatus of perception and
response, the logician with a world in which some classes
are magically not "null" and where he can, and does, say
so, where he must say so if a contradiction is to be anything more than a scribble on a paper, and where, of

course, no paper and no scribble are licensed to invade the purity of a formality that is the form of nothing because it is allegedly the form of everything.

The historical environment consists of monuments—that is to say, of what keeps us in mind. This is the energetic environment. It is artifactual. The passive environment is nature, the object of perception that is known "about." This passive environment has been the chief control of epistemology, the theory of knowledge. It must be obvious that any "theory" of knowledge begs the question. Economics has been called the dismal science because it appears to require scarcity, not abundance, not general affluence; well, where there is life there are at least passing moments of pleasure or bouts of dissipation. One could, in desperation, take to violence and revolution and make a noisy stir. At a minimum, this would furnish excitement, and it might even succeed. Heads have rolled. Compared with the self-annihilative implications of epistemology this is a glorious liberty.

But when it is supposed that in order to "know" one can only address oneself to the alien, to what, in principle, no demand of ours can ever constrain or modify, then knowledge becomes the medium of something less animated than misery. Some independence speaks in despair and rebellion. But vis-à-vis an environment that lacks all traces of mind and is required to show none in order to parade its independence and externality, knowledge has been doomed to the prison of subjectivism. In the end it has not even been possible to claim that there was a prison, as the object of knowledge reached out to enmesh even the alleged knower. When philosophy is charged with "speculation," it is for the reason that it made proposals about a region that is alien to thought and must be kept so if it is to be known "about." It has been necessary for philosophy to propose a region that would disqualify its own efforts in order to maintain the sense of effort. This is, in fact, a very interesting force in the history of philosophy and is not to be scorned. It is true that many do scorn the frustrations that are of their own doing. But frustration is also the sign of an essay in control, so that the radical rejection of frustration is also a radical passivity, a point that, with its consequences, the psychotherapists have not always acknowledged when they speak of being "adjusted" to reality of one sort or another. It is absurd to want to be adjusted to "reality"; it can make sense on occasion to come in out of the rain or to carry an umbrella, but that would depend.

Artifacts are not only themselves the vehicles of declared experience but are perceived only as part of the continuum of our own. That is why all utterance prolongs what has already been said and does not stutter to report an alien object of which no constitutional trace can be found in discourse itself. The entire epistemology that sees knowing as an attempt to pass beyond all appearance becomes irrelevant. It is by no chance, but by a fatality, that the theory of knowledge has concerned itself with a scientific rather than with a historical type of experience. The fatality occurs in the assumption that the object of knowing is no artifact, that it is a fact without being a factum.

23

The Facts

I do not wish to know more than, or less than, or as much as, Professor J——. That is not the point for me. I wish to join a community of learning.

How to practice such community is the question.

I am not distressed over the possibility of *ending* with facts; I am distressed over the claim that one *begins* with them in a scholarly discourse.

Purposes require the facts; science has none that are not part of its own procedure. There are no facts, not themselves determined by the procedures of physics, with which physics deals. Physics is not an interpretation of prior or independent facts. Nor is any scholarly discourse.

No scholarly discourse is a superstructure built on the alleged facts.

Wherever the facts make themselves prominent, something has happened to the adequacy of a discourse itself. Thus one finds emphasis on the facts of geology if one has been talking like Archbishop Ussher. Then one hears it said, "But *the fact is* that these rocks are more than 4004 years old." What is actually in question is not any facts but a type of discourse, for there is no Cambrian period except in geology. There is no such science as geology that interprets facts about rocks.

In the abstract, discrete facts suggest no story whatever. Because of that, the views of experience that have proposed such facts are rejected as nonsense. Such alleged facts cannot even be identified.

In teaching a skill a teacher may say to the learner, "Take my word for it; if you invert the divisor and proceed as in multiplication, you will get the right answer in the division of fractions." To learn that is to learn a skill; it is not to understand arithmetic. Early on, I vaguely resisted.

Some say that it is "impossible" for me to dispute J—— on Napoleon in so far as J—— has facts. I agree. But I agree not because he knows and I do not, but because there are no such facts. This is not to say that I know as much about Napoleon as J—— or plenty of others; it says only that the facts and the means of accepting, questioning, or rejecting them occur in what is said about Napoleon. A lawyer tests the credibility of a witness by hearing his story. When what is said lacks integrity, one doubts. When what is said violates the assumed community that any story requires, one doubts.

To propose a listing of facts before one writes, or hears, history is impossible. Every story assumes a shared background. No history could be written if every item had first to be independently known. Did Leonidas, a Spartan, fight at Thermopylae? But was there a Sparta? Where? Were there Persians? New information fits the unverified old and at some point must conform. That furnishes a critical basis to the reader. Further, such a basis is essential to interest and relevance. One reads best, and with maximum interest, where the assumed background is clear, where it is invoked.

I suggest that facts are sought where a discourse breaks down. Then one pauses to find means of resuming continuity. We get the facts we need, and we need none apart from an arrest. There is no peculiar authority in such needed facts except for the storyteller. A reader or listener does not want every statement to be presented as the resultant of a problem. That is impossible if there is to be any actual discourse. Action of any sort cannot be entirely deliberate. Deliberation is itself an episode. When evidence for some fact is scant, a writer will sometimes say that he regards such and such as likely. In so doing he shows the role of the fact as an item called for by a story.

A reader tends to accept as fact what the story needs for the telling. It is the story that empowers the reader to accept the facts. It gives him also the means of doubting. The writer himself furnishes those means.

Just as a common-sense matter, I would suggest that nobody will believe that no fact of Professor J——'s can ever be questioned unless, like him, one first puts in five or twenty-five years of investigation. Even the historian's facts need to lie in the common domain of reason and sense.

A decent discourse empowers and invites criticism. I suggest a distinction between ability to tell a story and ability to appraise it. Inability to tell does not imply inability to appraise. There is no factual bomb shelter.

What a dunce a man must be who confuses the facts with what he can find out! Such egotism! The facts are there, plain as a post, whether you know about them or not, whether you admit them or not.

I don't find any sense in saying that George Washington ate bacon whether or not anyone can tell. What about Washington? Did *he* have to tell? Could he? Let me board you for ten dollars a week and I will serve you bacon every morning—the kind of bacon that you eat whether you see it or not. I should really have been a businessman. See if you can get me some customers, the kind that feel they have had a good breakfast on the sort of bacon I serve whether or not they can ever find out whether or not I served any. A bonanza!

Business? Say rather, politics. Why, I should be in Washington city, telling people about the abundance of bacon on their tables whatever may be their views on the matter. A plethora of bacon. How misguided is the public, clamoring for bacon that is—or is not—all about them whatever they may happen to think. Vote for Miller and bacon, the bacon with tangy goodness, the new-processed bacon that is served every morning to all the underprivileged—or is not served—whether you think so or not. Patent applied for. Trademark registered. The Department of Justice would be impotent. Suppose they came around charging fraud. To be sure, I'd produce no bacon for them to see. So what? It would still hold that you had your bacon—or did not have it—whether or not the revenuers found evidence that you had bacon or had no bacon. I would be unworthy of my craft as a philosopher if I did not send them away completely convinced that the facts had nothing to do with their petty subjective findings, mere things of the mind, after all, mere ideas, and quite irrelevant to the hard reality where you either did or did not have bacon whatever their vain theories about the authority of their transient subjectivity.

That is the quintessence of the "real," to be there—or not to be there—whatever one may think. Abandon thought all ye that would enter here.

24

Order and Disorder

It would subordinate history to the ahistoric if one were to read the past as exemplifying a pattern not itself defined by time and discovery. Contrariwise, one could not expect to perceive any enduring pattern where the succeeding moments were discrete, atomistic, unorganized. Complete lack of order generates no order.

On the side of order, however, one meets the parallel problem of an absence of any disorder. This was the problem of the perfectionists. Pure being seemed not to fit actual finitude marked by ignorance, error, evil, suffering, or, for that matter, by pleasures and delights either. Heaven has not been represented as a locale favorable to comedy any more than for tragedy.

The consequence has been that one meets disapproval whether one asserts a total order or a total lack of order. People draw off if one enunciates an "eternal verity." And many are no better pleased if one rejects such controls of action or belief. In this standoff one is likely to be met with the familiar plague on both your houses. The whole matter is dismissed as mere futility. And why not fall in with that? For my part, I hesitate to treat any articulate utterance so abruptly. Plato with his "patterns" may be a fool, but folly itself becomes interesting when it has made itself articulate. Treat such attraction as a weakness; still, what could one say against it unless one borrowed patterns in the saying? The rejection of order conceals a pretension to another totalitarian command which, if it is to observe an inter-diction of patterns, cannot be articulated.

Patterns and atomicity: where does one stand in making the distinction? And also, where does one stand if one rejects the distinction? The aversion to "metaphysics" is the sign of an inability to identify the basis both of the distinctions and of their rejection. History reverts to phenomena if ahistoric patterns are in control. But what is in control? We want order, but not too much. We want some disorder, but not too much.

What is the status or authority of such sentiments? Are they mere vagrancies?

Cutting lots of corners, I suggest that such attitudes derive from the actual, from the limited and individual. That is where we are when there is neither controlling pattern nor complete disorder.

What one can learn from the historical past becomes the factors of self-maintenance. What those may be, only a present can discern or acknowledge. A person not now concerned in self-maintenance can learn nothing from the past as historical. He can learn only technology.

As self-maintenance the present is absolute. But it is also structured. What animals do not maintain is themselves.

But this present is also confused, not merely ignorant. To imagine a present without ignorance is to play God. Confusion is a matter of form, not of content; of order, not of more or less fact. We preserve our confusions. We exercise control through structures, but do not have a complete organization of structures. For example, in the view of psychology, how can there be history? In the view of physics, how can there be psychology? In the view of natural science, how can there be action, desire, aversion, virtue, or vice?

A completely composed actuality is impossible. So too is a completely disorganized actual present.

The historical past sharpens a present identity. In so far as Rome represents an essay in self-maintenance, we can discover what view of themselves the Romans had, whether it is also ours, and whether such a view is self-sustaining. We ask about formal constituents, those that gave form and energy, the very energy that also failed. In so far as I have another man's problems of form, I am not analogous but actually identical. It is this identity of actuality that is also our only community.

All form develops from the spontaneous. We will not abandon those spontaneities that lead to organization, hence to local control.

25

The Common and the Unique

Analogy is a form of induction. Each of two has certain properties; hence another property found in the one will also be found in the other. This is a risky inference, but useful as a guide to further inquiry.

Analogy operates in similarity or in the "common" quality, in the repeatable. Technology requires repetition. Physicians have "cases." A "common" noun requires examples, or instances. Conservatively: the common noun offers no barrier to repetition. It excludes the unique, which may not be repetitive.

Purpose-control operates on the analogous or repeatable. One saws *a* board, drives *a* car—the indefinite article. "Common sense" is the sense of such similarities, of a plurality with at least some properties indistinguishable in both or all. We are urged to show a common sense. Failure to use the common sense is a vagrancy and leads to damage. One uses common sense in driving an auto; one treats the act as controlled by *an* auto, *a* road, *a* set of brakes.

The definite article, in contrast, has been neglected. *The* so-and-so differs from *a* so-and-so. We have had no generally accepted place for the unique.

But the unique if viewed as quite separate from the common becomes inarticulate. The classic instance is the transcendent deity to whom no property common to any other object applies. It becomes "ineffable," not to be spoken of.

The problem is posed by the assertion of an *articulate*

uniqueness. How is that to be uttered? Is the unique unutterable? If so, what becomes of history?

The unique cannot, then, be entirely dissociated from the common. (Nor the common from the unique. But that is another story.)

The element of the common in the unique is what are called the facts. The past cannot be wholly dissociated from the present if one is to come upon a past. Trees, hills, streams, weather—eating, fighting, dying—are common to 1977 and 1777. The Saratoga surrender document, if there is one, is the same piece of paper. That assumption has to be made. It may turn out a deception, but it has to be made about that paper or about a similar object as the price of declaring a possible forgery. Otherwise one is dealing in clairvoyance.

But that there was an assembly of arms at Saratoga, that a fight took place, is not a fact, nor is it accounted for by the facts. Nor, if it were another fact, an instance of common sorts of objects, would there be any necessity of finding the event important. One ignores most of the common world. One minds one's own business and if one lives in Maine one grows potatoes and remains ignorant of figs or oranges. One could live in Maine and be more interested in lobsters than potatoes.

The facts occur in chronology, like the blizzard of '88. In that year there was *a* blizzard, but not the only one on record.

In a chronology the facts are accounted for ahistorically, as consequent on other facts. Science does that. A non-scientifically explained fact may be theologically explained. In these ways one accounts for the blizzard of '88, some favoring each method.

A chronological factor appears in any historical past. As children we learn "about" the past as if it were to be understood in contemporary terms. The past is viewed as a present possibility. Others have built a log cabin; so may I. More of them used to be built. In terms of common sense there is no alternative to such a view of the past.

But the Parthenon causes difficulty. We ask who built it

and decorated it. Some who were not as we are. Yet there are contemporary features about the Parthenon. It is *a* building, made of *a* material called stone or marble, on *a* solid base of rock, the upper part well supported, and so on. It has certain dimensions. All that is common. But that the building is there at all, and in that form, is so remarkable that we may attribute it to inspiration from the Muses.

What interest has one in the unique, in the absence of the common? People do not always relish being credited with common sense, being understood and accounted for only in terms of the repeatable. There is a difference between training and education. Men are "trained" for a new job as if their repute with others and their use to themselves consisted in meeting repeatable requirements. Proper names often derive from function, but function at earlier times gave distinction in a society. One was Butcher, Baker, even Miller, Fuller, Weaver, Shepherd, Wainwright, Taylor. One was *the* Miller in those days. Now occupation has become separated from the person, or rather, the person is lost in the occupation, not socially distinguished by it. The stenographer is displaced by the dictaphone.

Persons are not identified by analogy—that is, recognized as individuals in that form.

The past, like the person, is lost in so far as it is described and accounted for in repeatable terms. Technical problems do repeat. It can be desolating to say "Ah, yes, you are young"; or "You are old, Father William"; or "It seems you are in love"; or "You speak like *a* scientist" or ". . . *a* philosopher" or ". . . *a* Vermonter." On the other hand, one also runs dangers in treating others as individuals not to be confined to a type, but ready to deal with an idea in some freedom.

What can be dealt with as repetitive is technological. It assumes a continuing state of affairs. Now is again the time to raise taxes, to lower them, to raise or lower the discount rate. We can learn from the past in so far as it offers typical illustration. But that is not the unique historical past. Still, as above, there is no past at all unless some conditions and problems are typical and common. The absolutely unique has no past and summons none for its understanding.

The name I associate with an attempt to make the decline of states and societies a repeatable occurrence is Spengler. He has a scheme for it; history is ahistoric.

Where does one, then, drop anchor? First one needs a person who does not define himself analogically. Only the unique can discern the unique, or needs to. Individuals have an affinity for each other. The mind in career seeks an objectified career in persons and in institutions and is more at ease with itself; self-revision is nothing solitary. It comes to be noted that it is in career, in self-revision, that the not-self is most surely found. No one person invented English speech. The language is no private state of mind. And it is also the chief actuality of controlled revision. Within linguistic coherence words have changed their meanings. What one means personally by "good and evil," "true and false," derives from prior utterance. A language is a career in utterance. One's own nonrepetitive and individual actuality occurs as one is identified with a process for which there is no analogy. English is not an event in a factually predetermined environment. No one who spoke Latin, Greek, Sanskrit, or Anglo-Saxon could read off the English of today.

So, in so far as one hesitates to view historical events analogically, one is required to find both in oneself and in the not-self a nonanalogical order. As matter of fact the unique is not to be observed. It is found in a process of self-discovery. That neither oneself, nor another, nor nature, appears as a fact among facts has long been notorious. And the consequence has been that all three have been rejected as nonsense, as metaphysical nonsense.

The progress of an individual consists in part in the rediscovery of past experience. To the individual, questions about his identity are as fresh as they ever were. If I have skeptical proclivities, someone may smile and say that he once passed that way, or that Descartes did, or Protagoras. What saves my condition from the status of a factual or objective repetition is the medium in which it occurs. In that medium—discourse—the skeptical question is inherent. As much as Euclid, I can deal with a problem in plane geometry. If we share a problem, it is because of a discourse made in terms of lines, planes, angles, equality. The problem is there, not in Euclid or in me. I do not have an analogous problem, but the same one.

The problem in geometry is constitutional. If I want to saw a board, I can profit from another's experience. But there is no royal road to geometry. Not even the king can live in a geometrical order merely because Euclid did. Nor can I avoid such inquiry on the ground that the matter was settled by Euclid.

But is one not to say that in such cases—the skeptic, the geometer—I am in the same position as others? Can I not learn from them? Yes, I am in the same position, but I cannot learn from them. I must go through the problem myself. With respect to that problem we are not separately discoverable, treating the problem as an episode in separate individuals who may or may not share that problem and the discourse that generates it. These are not problems of circumstance.

Today people are like Ptolemy. They want answers and learned men who supply them. But they do not want to identify with the discourse in which the problem itself can be posed, without which it cannot even be posed.

In political history there is a problem of the decline of power. "Kingdoms rise and wane." Others have waned. So may we. Can one not learn from analogous cases? If there are "cases" and if they are analogous, then no one is identified through either. The problem is then technical. I happen not to want to see American power wane. Perhaps I can learn from Rome of the second and first centuries B.C. But perhaps a Frenchman wants to see our power wane and he avails himself of suitable techniques for attaining that desirable end. The Roman experience can be used both ways if one views it as a technique. External interests determine to what use a technique is to be put.

Our interest in Rome, as in geometry, assumes an activity that is not accidental but definitive of the political identity. The republic (*res publica*) is in danger. With respect to maintaining the republic our self-definition is the same. We can learn from the Roman failure provided the problem is not viewed technically. We have to ask, rather, what view of themselves the Romans entertained when they spoke of a *res publica*. For the Romans too were maintaining themselves, not using techniques to accomplish a coolly defined end to which they were external.

It is also worth noting that an American interests himself in the decline of Rome or Athens. Why not in the decline of Assyria or Egypt or Israel? It is because our political identity came through Athens and Rome. The very word "politics" is Greek, not biblical. Their career is also ours.

Thus what may seem analogical is actually a search for identity. We ask, "Who were the Romans?" We join them in self-definition, not in a technical problem. By knowing them better we know ourselves better. We profit not from a technical skill or failure, but from the common political purpose that is self-disclosing.

So I conclude that one is here dealing not in analogy, but in a career. We are together in a career, not as technicians.

26

Action and Immediacy

One never acts from a passive position, though one deliberates, and deliberation seems an arrest, a static condition of choice, a suspense.

But the suspense is kept up only in so far as the choice needs to be made. When a choice is not the extension of an attitude or program already adopted, one flips a coin or one skips it for something more intimate. Nobody can be troubled with choices in general. There are too many. One is concerned with one's own. And what makes them one's own is their furtherance of an action already under way. That restricts choices.

If in a more radical way one postpones action or tries to remain neutral to it, one finds it increasingly difficult to act at all. One withdraws, and that is pathological.

There is no criticism without spontaneity.

Yet it has often seemed that the spontaneous needs to be brought to judgment. If not, it seems arbitrary and lawless. This is the subjective analogue of the view that all events must be absorbed into the one causal order if they are not to be become anarchic.

It is true that the spontaneous is always open to criticism in point of content. But the critique of a content is never in terms of form alone, whether in ethics or logic. Form by itself tells no tales about specific content. Arithmetic does not tell one how much money there is in the bank. So the element of the spontaneous is always present as the price of judgment.

The spontaneous in being criticized is only getting established in principle. One looks for that spontaneity which is generative rather than arresting.

Now this is curious; it is the flavor of the modern world against the medieval and ancient. There, what was sought was restraint so as to prevent vaunting ambition (hubris) and self-regard (sin). Now, what is sought is the generative spontaneity, that being wrong or evil which bars access to nature, to man, or to any revision of our ideas of either.

But also, there is no identifiable spontaneity without criticism, provided that the criticism is not purely formal. One cannot find the occasion for criticism, for its need, for any threat to order, unless there is some order. But this order must also be more than merely formal. If I say it is 150 miles to Boston, there is no need and no way of criticizing that statement until one is already involved in travel and road maps.

Thus one is always in history, in action. And so one is concerned with consequences and with criticism. Criticism is the form of the immediate, and it is immediacy possessed of form.

Men of action are absorbed in what they are doing. They must sanction the present.

When they are confronted with the reflective mind, they are likely to take alarm and dislike. In that they are correct in so far as the attitude of thought is absolute and unsuited with action, an essay in occupying a position of complete aloofness.

But the "man of action" is to some extent uneasy and vulnerable. He does not, as a rule, really believe in action and in history. He is likely to be a conservative in the sense of supposing that his action falls within a world to which his action is appropriate. So, while he mistrusts external and aloof criticism, he is likely to invoke it, and to fear only the "wrong" sort of externality.

The person who fears externality most is the one whose capacity to act at all has been challenged or frustrated so that he perceives life slowing down and even losing its critical power unless there is freshness and spontaneity. But many of us have been brought up to fear all spontaneity, seeing there an acceptance of the actual which seems to put us too closely into life and finitude, and to remove us from that aloofness which is the alleged purity of the soul.

27

The Free Act

Activity without history may be egoistic. One attracts notice. One gets one's way. All action means some attempt to have one's way. But such action is subjective. It need not go on. One's own way is aimless. There is no order to desires. What begins as accident and as the arbitrary has no necessary continuity. It has no criticism of itself; and if a critic appears, there is the question of his authority.

Activity may be compulsory, not truly one's act. The slave cannot act. Freedom is the chance to act. To act is to create consequences. To act freely is to endorse consequence in principle.

The free act is the one that proposes systematic consequences.

All the talk about freedom fails in so far as action has not been presented as having consequences formally accepted. No free act can occur in a closed environment.

There is no systematic consequence until the act is more than subjective. It must occur as a sign of an order. But this order is also sustained by the act. An act that does not sustain and express an order of nature is only a subjective one. It has a closed environment. It falls within one's world and is explained in terms of what that world happens to be.

Action seems to need a future. Where there is no future in an act, or in a supposed act, there are no consequences, and so there is no importance. The importance of an act must, of course, be "formal." Does an act have form when it has no consequences? Is not the form the formal consequence? What can be meant by a formal consequence? Not anything specific. The formal consequence can only be the future.

The future is the formal consequence of action. Without action, and so moral and free action, there is no future. That there be consequences means that there be a future.

Consequences are important because they must be taken into account. But why must they? Why not evade them? One can evade specific consequences; one can move away, or pay a fine, or bribe someone not to be angry. But an act must have unavoidable consequences. One must live with one's act; it sets loose some nemesis, the sign that an act cannot be undone, that one must go on living with it.

Of course acts have always been seen as having some consequences. But an act was an offense against "nature" or against God, not against its own condition, its own possibility as act. Cain in killing Abel was not behaving in a way to make action possible. Loneliness, hate, leave us not with a man, but with a deteriorating mind, a deteriorating society. When the consequence of an act is the disruption of society, a breach of its laws, and a denial of its mode of self-definition, then the act has systematic consequences. It denies its conditions.

Where the consequences are external, they appear as arbitrary—the will of God, Paul's version of the law. Also, where the consequences are external, the motivations are likewise accidental and impulsive.

External consequences can be avoided. They do not depend on the act. The external forces may change, as in the case of God's mercy, a readiness to forgive and redeem for no reason external to himself. Or God may be influenced by sacrifice.

Thus the act is of no consequence because it literally has no outcome in itself.

Where the human act is not allowed to be absolute, it can have no absolute consequences. Its consequences will be in the power of those forces which permitted the act to occur.

It should be clear, too, that to deny that the act is free—that is, absolute—is necessarily to assume some more-or-less articulate condition in which it appears, such as nature or God. Neither, of course, can be defined in that case by invoking the act. Neither can be explained or understood through an act. Thus one should not make nature empirical, or define God through recourse to our own volitional experience.

28

Power

"Advances" in history can mean only advances in power. This will always appear as greater facility in carrying out purposes, such as transportation, communication, medicine, defenses against nature and against human enemies. Certainly, without such detailed and particular skills no advance can be claimed. Power means control in particular ways. A purely abstract power over man and nature defines withdrawal into trance.

Since all power is manifest in particular ways, it is easy and natural to conclude that such advances sufficiently define the meaning of history. Such a conclusion would be mistaken. Particular advances occur in a setting of the definition of power. Not all men have the same eagerness to overcome space and time, to advance public health or the art of the dance. It is not an easy matter to induce an individual, not to say a whole people, to modify its conception of the character of particular powers. Making a living attracts more people than the study of abstract economics, through which one's particular habit of earning a living may be criticized to one's disconcertment or possible private disadvantage. Then, too, some may feel that there is a larger residual power in art or religion, leading them to a neglect of economics as a study, or even to personal irresponsibility in money matters. There are those who see power in propaganda and in the psychological manipulations of individuals and associations. To advance in power is to advance also in the view one has held of how power is to be secured in particular ways. Parliamentary procedure and good logic are also ways of power, yet it may be very difficult to secure respect for them among persons eager for quick results, impatient of delay, conciliation, and criticism. Going to school is often regarded as a way of securing power. An educated people seems more powerful than an ignorant people. Yet general education with its delays and asceticism is not always welcomed by the individual or made a primary point of public policy.

History is an advance in power, but all such advance depends upon views of where power lies. A society develops such particular powers as its conception of the nature of power permits. Perhaps Americans see power in "the almighty dollar," the British in remaining "a nation of shopkeepers," the Germans in mysticism, the French in logic, the Latins in aesthetics, the Jews in fidelity to their ancient laws and usages. A nation is an embodiment of the articulation of some mode of power. Not all see power in the same way, as in education, science, religion, art, or free institutions. There are different emphases and different roads, often with a mistrust of other persons or associations whose views of reality or personality appear at variance.

History includes the disclosure of new modes of power. It is this which defines its revisory and revolutionary status. It is always difficult for the individual or for an association to modify its conception of the general status of reality with respect to which particular powers find development. For this reason a slight upon a man's work, his profession, or his associations, whether religious or secular, is a serious matter, disconcerting, and consequently an occasion for deep hostility.

29

Might and Right

"Might does not make right; it makes history."

This is true in so far as no right is established without might, and no advance in the conditions of right can be won and held without might. The ideal must be established in the state, and the state is force as well as reason.

But force by itself does not make history. Animals fight; lions keep on eating zebra meat, but do not thereby make history. The feuds of miners in the Alaska gold rush established nothing. Some force expresses and perpetuates anarchy. The force that makes history is a force on the side of law. The mistrust of force arises from the feeling that force is the agency that destroys law and reason, that it is the instrument and vehicle of anarchy and of the arbitrary. Thus force is regarded as the antithesis of the history-making process.

On the other side, reason without action is nerveless and ineffective. History seems in the keeping of those who go beyond reason and law by proposing to bring law and reason to pass. They can be brought to pass only as the outer and practical conditions for their exercise can get established. For reason is always imperfect, and the form in which it can occur and thrive is also always imperfect. Reason is the composition of differences, and the technique for doing that will vary. Force is the will to establish the outer instruments for the possibility of reason. When force is other than that it destroys history.

Thus history is the locus of the application of force directed at the establishment of conditions for the rule of reason. Force makes history where the intention of the force is historical. Arbitrary force makes history by disclosing the destructiveness not of force, but of the arbitrary. Hence, it is met by other force. Only as these two types of force meet can the idea of history become associated with the idea of force. For two anarchic forces neither make nor suggest the idea of history.

History is not moral: it sets the stage for particular moral systems. The advances of history are always and necessarily accompanied by force. Its setbacks may also be accompanied by force.

There is no moral judgment upon history. A moral judgment expresses the possible, an act launched from an outlook, where the determination of the act is in question. But one cannot question history. It is finished, as much so as nature. Morality is a concept of the relatively static. It assumes action within an outlook. It does not apply to the revision of outlooks. That revision is the redefinition of the moral, its establishment, not its detailed execution.

Morality is prospective. In terms of some present outlooks Jacob was immoral in having two wives and many concubines. But that is to shift position, and to ascribe to Jacob a code which he did not possess, and in terms of which his particular acts could not be judged.

This is analogous to aesthetic judgment. One does not judge Greek art by our standards. One places the Greek conception of beauty. In so doing, one cannot condemn, for that conception is a factor in the possibility of one's own.

The triumph of the North was not on the battlefield. Were slavery the avenue of history, did it describe the possibility of growth and of endless action, the physical victory of the North would collapse of its own feebleness, and slavery would come back—assuming that there *is* history.

To a man who still believes that slavery is the avenue of growth, the victory of the North must be ephemeral. It will be undone. It will develop internal weakness. To see the victory of right in the success of the North is already to have taken a stand as to the meaning of history and the character of winning forces.

But to say that the North is right because it won a physical victory is to abandon the idea of history and to lose a point of view for raising the question of whether or not might makes right. There then could be no question, and hence no meaning in the equation of might and right. To one depending on might alone, no question of right could occur.

The point of view which judges that the Civil War ended in right is not one separated from might. It is only the point of view of a differently intentioned might, not a point of view standing outside all might and making an absolutely intellectual appraisal.

Morality without force is as formless as force without morality. The former decays into inaction, and the latter into arbitrary action, and hence again into lack of will and discontinuity of deeds. They are dialectical.

Thus the triumph of right is not by accident associated with the triumph of might. In no other way *could* it triumph. But it is a triumph only because the very force that is defeated finds a stronger basis of affirmation of force, a more considered, a deeper, a more axiomatic and passionate basis in the intention of its victorious rival.

The problem of force is thus the discovery of the basis for its maximum exercise, its most abandoned and whole-hearted use. That, I think, is the real triumph of force. For force to triumph *in principle,* it must be used in the interests of a maximum egoism. And in the long run the maximum egoism will find the instruments of success. It will have them prepared as part of its way of life.

30

Action Is Inherently Historical

We feel tolerably sure that nature presents an orderly system of objects and laws. It used to be said that the regularity of nature needed to be assumed to make science possible, and scientists claim that they can predict events, at least in the controlled conditions of the laboratory, and by extension in the great world around us. Knowledge itself is sometimes identified with prediction, since where we do not know how to bring things to pass or how to prevent their happening, we do not understand their properties and their laws. Control is the evidence of knowledge. One knows so far as one can do. And certainly it would seem odd to claim any knowledge of nature if one could bring nothing to pass.

The great prestige of natural science is related to this direct experience of power. Considering their accomplishments, scientists tend toward modesty. This may be due, in part, to the impersonality of nature. We are likely to show emotion where we think ourselves put upon, crossed in our purposes or in some way kept from attaining our aims. Nature, however, pursues no ends contrary to ours, and rather rewards our inquiries than rebukes our trespass. It lends us the forces that we have the wit to employ, and our credit is never withdrawn except for laziness and ignorance. Only let a man catch a fish or grow a pumpkin and his triumphant smile will appear in the local press along with his trophies, and if he drifts on a raft from the Battery to Bedloe's Island he will write a book about it.

Nature seeks no chronicle, but man does. Perhaps this need of personal notice should be held against us. Yet it is not usually to our discredit that, like Don Quixote, we sally forth to seek fame, especially when the search involves danger and hardship, and is spurred on by devotion to some Dulcinea. What is morality if personal realities are to be disregarded and the promise of achievement goes unencouraged in our children and friends? Nature in its imperturbable neutrality may not honor the scientist, but his fellow men will erect a monument to Galileo in Santa Croce.

By action we undertake to make a world of our own. We become egoists and encounter the egos of others. Nature gives us infinite scope, yet even so, we must have telescopes properly housed, and apparatus to our hands that these hands have made. We must be equipped with artifacts if we are to discover the facts. Nature itself is not what we see and hear unaided. Its order, without which we do not identify it, is the order of these symbolic instruments, these functioning objects, which are the actual representatives of its structure. Nor is our morality a thing of the woods and desert, but of customs and institutions that do not aim to achieve an abstract good, but are the actual forms of whatever good we know and the occasions of the crimes that we can commit. We speak in words and in all manner of symbols, and are otherwise mute, unapproachable to others and excluded from their notice. Nature does not act at all, and animals react, while man acts because he takes into account what has been done.

Psychology has not been at all clear on the idea of action, and not infrequently it aspires to be considered a natural science studying the changes of alleged organisms when bells ring, lights flare, and electric currents annoy. But human action is addressed to action, to artifacts, to what has been done. Our learning consists in the modification of artifacts. When we merely use them, treating them as we would natural objects, we become barbarians, and force Ortega to write a book on *The Revolt of the Masses,* the new barbarism in which beauty, institutions, and the delicate products of science are made to serve subjective desires, while the thought that inspired them and the noble labors that produced them go unacknowledged.

It is by action that we establish history. We take into account what has been done. What we say or do thereupon reflects the artifactual world.

This is a central quality of historical reality. If there is any human world at all, it is found in our true deeds and in their implications. History is the endeavor to be accountable to the record of actions. That is why the historian consults records, looking down from the Capitoline Hill upon the ruins of the Roman Forum, searching out the men and motives that had set up the Colosseum and the temple of Mars Ultor and those other forces that brought their present ruin. It is a question of what men have done with their own world, such as it may have been at a given time and place.

History looks to the past, but this is only the necessary corollary of its concern with deeds. There are no human acts in the present or in the timeless uniformities of physical nature. Show me an act, and I will show you that what has been done is being taken into account in this new actuality. It is not true that one can concern oneself only with present deeds, or with a future activity, leaving the dusty past to historians who don't know enough to let the dead past bury its dead. There is a deep impiety in all novelties that purport to ignore or to scorn what has been done, no matter how enthralling the vision of a future that they may summon. Such proposals, often decked out as idealisms, are to be censored not so much for a falsely presumptuous knowledge as for their inherent failure as action. They do, indeed, appeal to nature, or to some truth, but in that context we do not act at all, but stand as the victims of a world that is not our own.

History, in this respect, is an attitude of piety. It is our reconciliation with the conditions of our own endeavors. It is the story not only of acts—*res gestae*—but of their condition. Moral theory has floundered about a good deal trying to find the "good" act, as if the goodness were an added quality, not definitive of action but accidental to it. The results have been bewildering and amazing, and never convincing. There is "virtue" in acting, and men feel this directly. Better a bad act than none. An actor is a pretender to human status, and if a thief takes my property he allows it to be mine, and has taken me into consideration in his disregard, as Hurricane Hazel does not when she knocks my chimney down. History is profoundly moral, and action, a consideration of what has been done, is beset by moral considerations in its defining pretension.

For these reasons we may hail the statement of Abraham Lincoln that "we cannot escape history." This inevitability is no summons to an *a priori* morality, as if we had to do good in the world. Slavery is a condition in which men cannot act. They must do what another requires, while the master is under no such reciprocal imperative. If one man may be enslaved, then there is no bar in principle to the enslavement of any man. There is no equation, then, between action and man, because there is none between man and man. We cannot escape history if we wish to avoid the paralysis of inaction. Action thereupon looms as the essential moral fatality. Lincoln was a kind man, and very likely a good man, but so are many others. There is no reason to think he was not a moral man. But none of that explains him. Indeed, many good men make a point of evading history. They think that in being good they may even escape its troubled finitude. He, however, stood for the essential condition of morality, namely, a chance to act for the slave, and no less a chance for the master. To lose the name of action was to lose the last best hope of earth.

31

Myth and Error

A myth is a story told in a way of telling that is inappropriate for telling the "truth."

Error occurs in the course of a way of telling that tells the truth. Science and research do not exclude error; they exclude myth. The ways of telling truth are inappropriate for telling myth.

Science excludes gods and heroes, purpose, final ends, values. What is less noted, it excludes an authoritative or controlling immediacy, a presence as a power.

Any story of any past resembles a myth in its way of telling. Whether Diana or English yeomen shoot arrows, the telling is indistinguishable in the common assumption of a local, a present, an active power. This identity of a way of telling a story in myth and in history has excluded history from telling the truth.

In so far as myth has been discredited it is not for the reason that another than Diana shot arrows. It is for the reason that the "true" account of the event excludes anyone from shooting arrows. Yet historians go on telling stories as if someone did shoot arrows.

History purports to exclude myth, and in that respect resembles science. But history does not exclude the way of telling a story that also characterizes myth. History does not say that Diana shoots arrows, but it does say that soldiers at Agincourt and Crécy shot arrows. Such a way of telling is not scientific. If it is historical, it is also mythological, the way of the *logos,* of a telling, of a mythical account.

So if the historian insists on having someone shooting arrows, he has to speak exactly like a myth-maker. Teucer, Philoctetes, William Tell, fade into myth. It is not that statements about archers are false rather than true; it is rather that such a way of telling is neither true nor false, but mythical. But the mythical way of telling cannot be avoided by the historian.

So if anyone wants history, he had better not reject stories regarded as mythical. He must join the myth-makers. What other way of telling can he adopt? Will he rather join the physicists or the psychologists? He cannot do so if he supposes himself to be telling that there were acts, heroes, rascals, victory and defeat, organization and decline. Homer presents Achilles and Hector; the historian presents Lincoln. There they are! As actors and heroes they are nowhere else to be found. Lincoln is one of few Americans to appear in hexameters or their equivalent. Repudiate the legend and you lose the hero. That is the consequence of the truth-telling.

If one had to choose between myth-ways and truth-ways, one would think it a hard choice. There seems no way of making such a choice on a responsible basis. Nor is there. But are truth-ways any less accounts of *action* than are myth-ways or history-ways? Is truth less *in the telling* than is the historical presence? Show me numbers, spaces, times, apart from the telling. I have elaborated on the yardstick as no perceptual object, and will not repeat.★ Truth also must be told. Nature is also a presence, and like the hero must be made to appear in an appropriate revelation.

Science tells truth, but only in terms of controls as purely active as the thunderbolt of Zeus. Science and history alike operate only in a prior actuality. Science is now discovering that it has a history and that it has heroes like

★See John William Miller, "The Midworld" and "Functioning Objects, Facts, and Artifacts," in *The Paradox of Cause* (New York: W. W. Norton & Company, 1978), pp. 106–29.—ED.

any other endeavor. I find it a bit comic that scientists are now rather shyly venturing into their history. Within the limits of physics there is no past, no dated time, but what those limits may be entails a career, proper names, and historical dates.

Homer's heroes may not be mine. Ptolemy's truths may not be mine. But in so far as I have heroes and truths I have ways of telling that are also theirs. Heroes change, and truths; but those changes are consequences of greater control in the act of telling. The shape of nature changes and also the shape of action, so that our truths and acts require a new telling. That Achilles and Heracles were once heroes requires the discovery of the mind of the times that saw them so. Show me any mind of a time and I will show what truth-tellers call a myth. Action and the springs of action end as no part of the truth.

History differs from myth in that historical acts redefine action itself. The world of Homer is static. Zeus is always the same. It came to be alleged that Zeus did not act as a "person" acts. Act moved into self-control. The gods lacked it. How one could claim to act became a problem. The men who raised it were the new heroes. The ancient answer was not, however, in terms of history, but in terms of a change in the static. So we have static "ideas," or a static totality. We came into history only as our totalities changed, and changed on their own terms. Our own "new birth of freedom" was a consequence not a displacement, a resultant not a "truth," a "birth" not an ungenerated matter of fact.

If one wants history, then a self-revision of totalities cannot be avoided. And no such revision is a truth. It often appears as an assault on truth, on the assumptions that regulate the truths we tell. It was so with Galileo and Darwin. They upset people in a way that Marco Polo did not, although he told very strange stories.

The hero, mythical or historical, embodies power just as gods have wielded power. But power is no constant quality, neutral to epochs and persons. It has been the case that the gods have been powerful and when proved not so have been abandoned as idols. As the sense of power changes, so do the gods; and where power is denied, all gods and heroes become less than illusion because meaningless. But differences among gods are also differences in what are regarded as powers. Even in Greece the sky-gods and earth-gods led to different practices and to different views of personal power.

It did not matter how power was construed. It always turned out to be a "myth," whether the power was that of Diana, Achilles, or Plato's cosmic workman. The anti-myth claim has had no stopping point short of the denial of power. Far from making us free, the "truth" has not been comfortable in allowing us to exist at all, let alone gods and heroes.

In the age of innocence, the Olympian age, power was not questioned. Of course there were powers. We call it animism. "All things are full of gods"—that is, of powers. The scientific and intellectual movement had the effect of abolishing local power, the power of Zeus hurling thunderbolts or of the wrathful Achilles. Power became organized or funded. It passed away from the local, from the magical object, the spontaneous individual. Today the claim to have acted is regarded as a relic of the prescientific magic. The intellectuals smile with superior knowledge and explain the act away into a non-act, into a funded uniformity. Sometimes even the funded uniformity gets rejected as smacking of a pretension to a present control. Then we have "pluralism," a view to which one can set no limit without the reinstatement of a personal control.

So gods and heroes have become the very marks of stupidity. They are myths. And they are mythical for the central reason that they occur as power and as action. Get rid of action and you also get rid of the hero. Any story, *any* story, of a world in terms of action then becomes a myth. Any account of events in terms of action becomes mythical. It is not "true."

We can hardly attempt to restore heroes in terms of truth. The true gods have turned out not to be gods at all, and for the very reason that they are "true," as truth has been conceived in its suspicion and, finally, in its rejection of local, present, immediate power. The truth is also our impotence. Our professors in universities seek truth, so they announce; where do they declare power? Any power is attacked and derided as a primitive stupidity, as superstition, as a myth. One should not be surprised at this turn of affairs. Truth reveals no will.

Radical passivity lacks inspiration. Discoveries develop from discipline and engagement. Art may be for the sake of art, a value in itself, asking no ulterior warrant. So, too, knowledge has been viewed as good in itself, but this does not carry the inference that one had been dozing in lethargy when determining that the area of a circle equals πr^2. Knowledge may be a "tool," but a tool has to be *made* and the tool-maker rates as a superior craftsman. Tools do not grow on trees. Common sense has not divorced action from its instruments, as if each appeared as an independent factor. In fact, it is a radical defect in psychologies of motivation that they look for action in the absence of those vehicles which carry out and formulate an impulse, drive, propensity, urge, instinct. If action were another "fact," why would one suppose that knowledge could get any hold on it? It is foolish to suppose that the nervous system, when viewed as a fact, has any more use for learning than the solar system. Nobody puts the solar system in the kindergarten. Action not already in the control of knowledge fades away into "reaction" where knowledge neither explains the act nor can influence it.

Instrumentalism is a remarkable abstraction. In order that knowledge be made "relevant" it destroys the conditions that would make it so. We should not blame undergraduates who demand "relevance." So do their teachers. "The rudeness that has appeared in me have I learned from my entertainment," as with Viola in *Twelfth Night*.

The instrumentalists left in total ignorance the impulses that were now supposed to make use of knowledge. So we put the nervous system to school and find the pattern of knowledge in the laboratory reactions of rats and birds. I do not find the egoistic surge of undergraduates surprising, nor the sorry wailings of the existentialists who find "No Exit." Well, of course, a room with no entrance has no exit either. If the occasion for knowledge is an impulse, and if, as with Freud, these impulses spring from a dark unconsciousness, then knowledge is a total alien to the state of affairs for which it is recommended as a tool. Instrumentalism is hoist by its own petard. It has been a source of our current demoralization. Even John Dewey wished for "the unforced flowers of life." Flowers, now, what use are they? So we had those unforced flowers, the "flower children," hardly avid for mathematics or physics, let alone logic or history.

is merely come upon, there nothing more can be claimed for the present, either. It, too, is merely come upon. Look at the shape of that state of affairs: I merely *come upon* my present; it is in no way definitive of me; by the same token, the condition of yesterday leaves me as I was before I had heard of it. In nothing that I come upon, whether past or present, is any constraint laid upon me, any compulsion, since all that I encounter could just as well be some other way. Nothing that lies in the area of history, of "things done," requires that I do anything in particular, or that I control what I may do by the laws and imperatives of any state of affairs resulting from acts not my own, acts that I merely observe and, for that matter, need not even observe. In terms of such an approach to *res gestae* no act of mine can be solicited or demanded by the state of affairs that happens to come to my notice. There is, indeed, a deeper result: Can I find by observation any act at all where, by hypothesis, no act of my own has been presumed in the observation? In a parade of appearances I am a spectator only, and in what I observe no compulsions appear. Where one merely observes, there no act is observed, nor any "necessary connection," as was shown by Hume, with consequences which appear in Kant, who tried to restore necessary connections.

Now, a reported act is a contradiction. In report, no act appears. To allege an act is to claim an event in terms of the structure of an outlook, of an intimacy between person and outlook, indeed of an identity of those two abstractions. To claim to have observed an act is to invoke what, to the agent, is no observation, but something so close that he can not divest himself of it. But in what way is the spectator, merely observing alleged acts, to find such a compulsion in a supposed agent? The spectator, the reporter, the observer, claims to be under no necessity. There is nothing he must report, nothing he must *omit* from a report. Any special interest on his part stands as arbitrary and subjective; for one it is Greece, for another the Renaissance. His very looking is not enforced by anything he sees or may see. He need not look at the past at all; he could just as well study math or physics, where no dated past is the content of what is being observed or a deliberate control of what is being done.

I sometimes think that historians, including historians of philosophy, are determined *not* to find any act in the past. A remarkable feature of the Church, as of other cults, is its artistic richness. How is one to account for all that? There is Chartres; Henry Adams says it was built by the Virgin, and so it was. But the Virgin, or Pallas Athena, is a "myth"—that is to say, unaccountable on common-sense terms, not empirically observed, not found among the objects or experiences to which we respond purposefully and for "terminating" results, as the pragmatists say. The curious feature of myth is its capacity to build a Chartres, a Parthenon, a nation, to give voice to song and story. Take away the myth and you take away much of *res gestae*—I would say all of it—leaving only the laboratory rats and pigeons. The great springs of action are myths, like Christianity, and all have some element of revelation or inspiration. Poets invoke the Muses, and even Lucretius invoked a divinity, Venus. What is the Second Inaugural without its declaration of the fateful, of the judgments of the Lord which are "true and righteous altogether"?

The springs of action have had a mythical force. The strong, persistent, and eloquent act appears as the enactment of the mythical order. It is also notable that a monument does more than state a fact; it summons to further action, the shrine or church to devotion, Independence Hall to the cause of free government. A monument is more than an appearance, one of many, no more demanding than any other object or, if arresting, then only as it suits a private and practical purpose, like a stone to be put behind the wheel of a cart or auto on a slope. A test of the historian occurs in the task laid upon him when he encounters a monument. What must he then do? If nothing, then I say he has not encountered an act, but only another object or appearance.

I have to make a broad statement: To encounter an act is

to encounter also what to the neutral positivist is a myth. I say, too, that while the ostensible objection to myth is its falsity or unreality, the actual objection is to its force as launching and controlling an act. Take away myth, or what is called myth, and no action can be found either now or in the past. The current objection to myth is the same as the long-developing objection to *any* controlling order. A *locus classicus* in modern times is the rejection of cause by Hume. The result appeared in a wholesale rejection of organization words. They were called pseudo-concepts and included personal pronouns. Acts have always had something mythical about them because associated with persons, with tribal or national identity, with *lares* and *penates,* or with Olympus. Such entities or forces have been denied reality. How does one say as a matter of observation and report, "He prayed to Zeus"? These are all dubious words if one insists on translating them into any content of consciousness. As supposed observers and reporters, historians themselves deny that any basis for observing a *person,* his act of *praying,* and *Zeus* can be found in the content of consciousness. The very basis of the historian's discourse—the act—is not to be observed. I remember J. P. Baxter warning against imputing motives. But the difficulty is not so much that a false motive will be imputed as that any motive at all invokes a basis of explanation that can never be observed. Impute any motive and you deal with what gets called a myth—the ego, the individual, the act, causality, rational control, the Olympians, the Trinity, heaven and hell. The more passionately controlled, the more mythical the act becomes, launched by a myth, and tenaciously persisted in because of that myth. Any supposed reportorial history has a built-in aversion to the act.

When Kant proposed to find necessary connections in physics, he had to find organizing terms that were not content of consciousness—space, time, cause, quality, quantity, and the rest. These were said to be assumed in all report of nature. Kant has been assailed. Such *a priori* assumptions were not empirical. The reporter had, for

Kant, an organization in terms of which he did his reporting. This reporter never appears among the items reported. He is a myth. Strict empiricism wants a report and no more; but it also wants no reporter. Let him appear, and the alleged report is criticized as his, as colored by him. Gibbon was, after all, a "rationalist"; to that extent his story is to be scouted.

History has no Kant to disclose the organization in terms of which all reports of action get told.

But can one any more observe actions than one can observe causes or energy or space or time, or any of the other modes of the organization of objects? If one repudiates all controlled immediacy, one also rejects all order in the stream of consciousness. In fact there is no "stream" and no "consciousness" to be found in absolute passivity. Such distinctions entail rejections not of errors but of a myth, the myth of the observer and his critical capacities. If there is no ego, one cannot say, "I find no ego." The unorganized reporter can "find" nothing. He doesn't *look* for anything. No present active participle—such as "looking"—can then be employed.

Radical empiricism commits no errors. But what is a "fact" if one cannot be in error; and what is an "act" if it can never be mistakenly interpreted?

In any act there is an element of an imperative, in one's own, and in the act of another. Nature shows no action; indeed, nature, as the region of objects, was revealed only as animistic accounts of change were supplanted by an impersonal, or nonpersonal, order. Today, any suggestion of imperative in an act gets viewed as a psychological compulsion, as a fixation or habit that is no longer at one's discretion. To say that one must now read a book, cast a vote, speak logically, greet a neighbor, is to give evidence of one's helplessness. One is said to lack an ability to "choose." And when the choice has been made, it is then claimed that some "conditioning" process has been operating. I would say that where action is seen as enlarged "choice," the agent seeks to retreat forever from any necessity, to stand aloof, to reject all direct engagements, to deny his equation with any state of affairs. Any such equation is regarded as evidence of helplessness. There is not even any necessity to take note of any state of affairs. What is it to me that there are Christians and Jews, capitalists and communists, or that there were Greeks, Romans, and the members of the Constitutional Convention? Is my liberty of choice to be denied by forcing attention? Must I pay attention to physics, history, art? Must I respect a neighbor's property? I find that such a demand is viewed with hostility, not because of any malice toward a neighbor, but because respect looms as a denial of option, of that aloofness to any act which the free man requires. The Christian who had to say his prayers, who had not to sacrifice to the gods or emperor, is then regarded as the victim of a myth. Similarly, if one has to mind one's p's and q's, or pay one's bills.

An absence of necessity in nature and in other persons leaves one's own conduct without requirements or organization. An unordered state of affairs, even when limited, leaves one at a loss. One does not know where to take hold. Action is summoned by what already has some shape. People speak of being at liberty to do as they happen to wish, but one's very wishes disappear in circumstances of disorder or, rather, non-order. Utter ruin, as in a war, paralyzes action, and when any can be undertaken it is from some base where not everything has been reduced to incoherence. We are stunned by calamity, and if we recover it is by falling back on some remaining patterns. The death of a parent or spouse or child can be unorganizing. But something is usually left, and around that residue energies can take shape again. A wife or husband dies, but perhaps a child remains to summon action and to give it direction. Suppose one enlarges unordered experience to the limit and says that none of it stands in a structure, in a shape, form, order. What, then, is to be done? Nothing— no one—recognizes one's effort, even the attempt. To do anything at all is to have recognized an environment that solicits, permits, demands, and controls an act. Such is the state of affairs when one is addressed in a language. A reply is solicited, it is made possible, it is demanded, by the acceptance of language, and it is controlled by the accepted vocabulary and grammar, by logic or other inherent structure. What one has encountered is not a chaos or a ruin, a mess of discrete sensations, none sequent upon any others, none proceeding from any prior manifestation, none leading to a sequel.

The empiricists did not begin with an attempt to evade all controls over presentation. They began, rather, with the hope of removing false or illusory controls. Descartes felt that he had often been "deceived," but he said so only as a preliminary to a search for reliable control. He hoped to avoid victimization, as did also the British empiricists. The ideal limit of nonvictimization would be found in utter passivity. In that way one has no prejudice. The so-called data pose no problem. They are not to be examined. One does not say, "Was that a hawk or a heron?" To ask such questions could turn one into an undecided Hamlet. The passive is not undecided; it makes no decisions and no judgments. Nor can it be summoned to action or to judgment by what it perceives. No question, no demand, is made by a datum received in all innocence.

"Hawk" and "heron" are common nouns, formalities. They exhibit the universal of the class name and so entail genus and species and much else. One has then moved out of passivity into criticism, judgment, inquiry, exploration, action. If it is said, "There is a hawk," one may shift position to look, or one uses binoculars. "Hawk" is an action word, as are all other common nouns. It is a vehicle of order. That order is no passive datum but a summons and demand. Shall one then call classification and all that it implies nothing but a myth? Is it a prejudice? Is the logical order of objects another illusion, and are we to say with William James, "So much the worse for logic"?

It is indeed curious that the pragmatists find no command in the circumstances that they encounter. For them action has no coherent order, because their circumstance has none. In our time it has come about that the order of objects is regarded as an obstacle to action, while, also, the need to act is strongly affirmed. In ancient times, and much later, circumstance seemed to nullify action, but action lacked the plausibility that it has now acquired in an age of technology and management. But to say that there is *command* in circumstance is to be charged with myth. A tremendous criticism has challenged and denied any order, any command, in circumstance, in the world around us. By the same stroke it has rejected the person as defined in terms of order and necessity. Composure is not found or permitted. Composure is said to inhibit spontaneities in a person, and to impose an alien order on circumstance. That the energy, the drive, the tenacity of action, depends on composure is then overlooked. That enlargement of power and exploration of circumstance require the energies of composition is forgotten. Rather, that energy entails composition and fails in atomicity of things and persons is not explicitly recognized. Still, even electric energy occurs as a polarity, as reciprocity, or as transfer. This, of course, was an ancient idea. Hot, cold, dry, and moist, one and many, odd and even, and other differences permitted a composition. Heraclitus called it strife; Hegel, the dialectic of opposites.

33

The Role of the Actual

The chronological past has no shape. It is all the events common to all points of view. The historical past has shape. It is not a common past. It is peculiar to each society, for each society has its own past as surely as it has its own present. The common past is possible only from a common present, and such a present is not a historical present, being the present of no one in particular and of no particular society.

Only the particular present has a historical past. Therefore the historical past will be as particular as its present extension. Hence the specific events of the past will be a necessary factor in history.

The Cooper Union speech is an attempt to define the American community. Not every community needs to make up its mind about slavery. Perhaps America did not need to. But here is a claim that the American community is not defined through slavery, that, in fact, it is rather defined through suspicion of slavery in so far as the specific words and deeds of the Fathers can bear witness. Of course there is an assumption, namely, that the country of the Fathers is also that of the people of 1860. If otherwise, the whole speech would become irrelevant.

Every community invokes its peculiar past. Where none is actual, one will be invented. Present will, present self-definition, can only continue past values. Some self-consciousness must be past if any is to be present. We never face *all* the past from the present. We face part of the past from a point of view already past, but viewing its own past. Lincoln appealed to the Fathers, who were past, but he did so because they were already in part self-conscious. For that reason alone could their testimony be of use.

Thus history is built in triadic relation. As Hegel would say, one must find in the object all properties of the subject. *Ergo,* look into the past for the pattern of reflection that one now applies to that past; look to the Fathers for the meaning of our own problem because they saw their problem as one of will.

Consequently, just because history is reflective and self-conscious, specific events become part of its meaning. Its meaning lies in the past occasions of reflection, never in an abstract present interpretation of a past viewed abstractly.

This concreteness of history is very central, I think, and the need of finding self-conscious change objectified in the past, if only in myth, seems to me constitutional. That is how the specific event enters history. It is the ancestor of the present will, and bone of its bone.

To be sure, no maker of history, no doer of any act, knows all its implications. Action advertises limit. But any self-conscious doer of any act does know that he is limiting the future, restricting it. He knows *some* of the meaning of his act. He knows, if he acts self-consciously, that God will see him, or that history will record his deed if only in a footnote or in some vaguer way.

Where a past act acquires a present "meaning," it can only be the act itself, the mood of the act, the spirit that produced it, that has been prolonged. An act gets reassessed by itself—that is, only by the same society which it defines and within which it operates.

Every act, I would say, shows at least a conscious purpose, and even a self-conscious one. If history has anything at all to do with acts, one can't very well deny that such acts show conscious motives or even self-conscious and history-making motives. Indeed, I would say that the rise of history is all the same as the rise of self-conscious restriction of the future. Its purposes become very clearly seen, because they are seen as secular and as infinite. An act embodies an unknowable nemesis. But even so, any self-conscious act on the part of a free community or its leaders will not escape history. It will always stand, at the very least, for the identification of an issue.

I would not want to make the historical event too much a function of its present meaning. I want the event in itself to be historical, so that it may be part of my self-definition in the historical community, or implied by known historical events of that community. An event not historical in itself can never become so apropos of history.

I feel sure that history is original, that we all begin as historians, equating ourselves with the past, and with a quite sharply specific past. It may be myth, but it will be there. In the abstract one can never ask, "What is my past?" That is a contradiction. My past is always there, and it is as specific as I am. There is no difference between an event in my historical past and the meaning of that event. One begins with history.

In history things need to have been really done. Lincoln must have spoken at Gettysburg, and spoken the words reported. It is a serious thing to disillusion anyone about his historical past—say, by calling it myth. It may take a long time for the poor devil to see that myth can never exceed reality, so that he does, after all, have something to live with. One needs a past. A historical past is more than a thing of time; it is always the bearer of infinity, the dynamic of divine forces in time. So I say one won't succeed in separating event and meaning, specific event and history. History will have the incarnation. The soul won't disavow the body or treat it as something to be given a meaning. It is precisely in history that truth becomes identical with the faiths of men. Truth has stepped down from eternity into time, and so into specific events.

34

Judgment

History, the study of past acts, has not been burdened by the weight of an over-all pattern of reason. Nobody has supposed that the life of action was, or could be, an exhibition of perfect control. In action one does what the situation calls for, and ultimate ideals play no direct part. Action is messy, averse to perfectionism, which, indeed, becomes inhibiting and therefore diseased. The man of action meets a specific situation, or a specific person, not the entire universe. There is nothing to be done about the universe. The simple reason for this occurs in the inability of all things—of a totality of things—to give relatively greater importance to one specific situation or person than to another. To act one must forget about an ideal totality and heat some water for coffee, even though the country is going to the dogs or the divine wrath is abroad in the land. Action is obliviousness to an ideal totality. It is improvisation. It is expediency.

In contrast with expediency stands abstract principle. Expediency without principle is anarchy, but principle without expediency is dogmatism. Dogma is the professed irrelevance of human experience to truth. The dogmatic man of principle poses as confronting vagrant expediency with a rule not derived from anything that man has been able to learn, much less to justify or make reasonable, through his limited and finite experience. Dogma is the indictment of the capacity of finitude to attain self-control.

It is always averse to self-control as an ideal. It is averse to freedom and to history. It is precisely the purpose of dogmatic principle to disqualify self-rule, and to impose a rule that draws its authority from its immunity to criticism. What good is a "principle" that has none but a finite sanction, that is capable of revision by the same processes that produced it? Consequently the man of principle will never invoke history. For him history is to be viewed as falling under a rule—the rule of causation if he is a materialist, the rule of God if he is a supernaturalist. In either case history has no reason in itself, no "immanent" reason, as the philosophers say.

Historians are among the more responsible men of our time. They are shy of any view of their subject that disparages the importance of what has been done in all the darkness of finite purposes. Nobody, of course, wants to view his own endeavors as trivial, but the historian is in a much more serious situation than the natural scientist in this respect. The natural scientist usually has an idea of nature, and he treats nature as an objective reality, self-contained and omnipotent over all changes among the objects of experience. He is dealing not in the personal but in the impersonal, not in the subjective but in the objective, not in the act but in the fact. In so far as psychologists claim scientific standing, they too see the act as related to the facts, to physiology, chemistry, physics, and so to that immense object called nature. Their reports are findings, and they try to view action as behavior—that is, as changes in the objects that are "organisms" when "stimulated" by other objects or situations. In all this the particular events observed enjoy the dignity of a status in an ideal order that the philosophical naturalist also views as the real order.

But the historian has no such cozy refuge for his materials and statements. He tells only about acts and about the dealings of agents with agents. Brutus murdered Caesar because Caesar was ambitious, not because Caesar suffered from a nervous disease called epilepsy, or because of any fact in nature, physiological or chemical. Plutarch tells about this celebrated event in terms of what people thought, not in terms of centimeters, grams, seconds, or volts. Antony offered Caesar the crown, but his refusal was applauded. "This," says Plutarch, "made the multitude turn their thoughts to Marcus Brutus." Brutus, however, remembered his association with Caesar and hesitated to lead a conspiracy. "For he had not only been pardoned himself after Pompey's defeat at Pharsalia, and had procured the same grace for many of his friends, but was one in whom Caesar had a peculiar confidence." This is the vocabulary of act, not of fact, of emotion and desire, not of yardsticks or clocks. It does not matter that Brutus may have misconstrued the motives of Caesar. Perhaps Caesar was more kind, or Brutus less disinterested, than Plutarch's story suggests. In any case the story is one of deeds done, and of what particular persons felt it necessary to do in a specific situation. Perhaps all this has a moral, such as that "pride goeth before destruction," but that is not what places these events in history.

History is not an edifying spectacle. It contains all the rascals as well as all the saints. It is a report on the states of mind that account for all these acts. This is the difficult position in which history finds itself. For who believes that states of mind and their attendant acts possess reason in themselves, and that they announce one of the defining modes of reality? In our time, especially, states of mind are not independent, free, autonomous, self-regulating. They find their rationale elsewhere, in some ideal scheme treated as also real, but itself immune to the taint of being only a state of mind. In these terms history is not only the record of follies but is itself a folly if it supposes that it can escape reduction to the ahistoric.

It is generally admitted that we cannot escape nature and, more particularly, nature as described by physics. One commonly finds the belief expressed that all phenomena of life will be reduced at last to uniform law, and that what now appears as unpredictable will at last fall within the invariant laws of physical nature. This belief, and this hope, apply to biology and psychology, and, through them, to all the expressions of man, including art, religion, and history.

Nevertheless, the confident rise of natural science has been haunted by the ever-present shadow of its own dependence on human inquiry and human capacity. The alleged impersonal world of nature, aloof from man, indifferent to his beliefs and hopes, reflects man's experience, his sensory equipment, his critical sense, and his demand that what befalls him shall have organization and clarity. It is indeed striking that the quite external and impervious world of physics should so soon have been viewed as a phenomenon, not as an absolute reality.

There is an original sin of the intellect, as of the will. Sin has been regarded as a severance from the absolute, a diminution of being, an absence of perfection. To propose that one shall find out the truth for oneself is to abandon passivity and docility for the sake of one's own judgment. In all its forms this is the humanistic tendency. It is the grand assumption of free societies. Physics itself is a product of this egoism, a fruit of man's own desire to know, and to judge. It was Aristotle's statement that man by nature desires to know; it is the sharper claim of modern man that he proposes to *judge,* being bound by nothing other than his own experience and by causes, standards, or methods that are themselves the fruit of experience and, in turn, receive justification only in their fruits. We rely on physics, but not for the reason that it absolves us of the need of judgment. Its great prestige has a different root, namely, its complete liability to revision through no better authority than human experience.

The shadow of humanism haunts our modern studies because we propose to make our statements responsible. We can help what we say. We can correct whatever we may say, and judge whatever we may do. These are the assumptions of a free society and of free men. When we disavow that responsibility, we take refuge in one of the characteristic modes of avoidance, namely, dogmatism, skepticism, or mysticism. All these have a common denominator in their suspicion of finite experience.

One should be careful not to confine dogmatism to theology. It has a good illustration in mechanistic naturalism, or materialism. The core of dogma is the disqualification of experience, and of finitude, no matter what the character of the absolute object within which it falls and of which it is a by-product. Confined to experience, we must either assert the equivalence of experience and reality or else consign it to the appearances of the inscrutable. The mystic, to be sure, does assert the equivalence of experience and reality, but only when his experience evades finitude and articulation. What he denies is the satisfactoriness of the relational, where completeness remains an ideal eternally postponed by the very forms of its apprehension.

Humanism offers no Nirvana, no period to inquiry, no final satiety. Spaces have no term, and time passes into a perpetual future. Causes reach before and after in infinite complexity. Our purposes lead on to more complex desires, and to the perpetual postponement of masterful poise. It is this radical incompleteness of all articulate thought and purpose that induces the mystic to take arms against a sea of troubles, and by the exclusion of all limited concerns to end them. Like the dogmatist and the skeptic he proposes to put an end to history.

Surely these are large issues. But can one cut them down to more comfortable size? Had we not best face the consequences of the claim to responsibility? One might, to be sure, settle for physics on the ground that it has furnished conveniences. But such a result is a form of obscurantism. It is an evasion of the responsibility of man to man. In our society we address each other, and although we may feel inclined to put our authority off on God or nature, we foul the lines of communication by such abdication. Devoted as we are to nature study and to the exact sciences of objects, we are no less devoted to the procedures by which statements get made. Our truths and powers are based on the prestige of truth-telling, and on the persons who tell it. The truth is something told and carries the liability of articulate justification. Our truth is a social truth. At the same time, it is not a monotonous and uniform doctrine, but rather a fabric woven of innumerable personal inquiries and acts, all responsible to the conditions of communication. It is these procedures, forever tentative and risky, sustained only by the energies of good will, that underlie the stubborn humanism of our time.

We stand in a historical position that condemns finalities to darkness or to illusion, the *ignis fatuus* of a destructive bog. We can hardly go back on our present position. It would entail not only the loss of further inquiry into nature but the more homely and more directly felt loss of our social reality. Our morality is that of recognizing the capacities of men for enlarged and responsible thoughts and acts. Our legislation is bent toward that enlargement, and our studies and associations are bent toward its responsible control. What seems so momentary has taken on the dimensions of the absolute. It is not too much to say that disrespect for the present moment of experience in the individual has become our version of that primal eldest curse, a brother's murder. We are not respectful of men because of their status in some eternal reality. We are respectful because they now endeavor to order their lives in work, play, and expression, and because they seek ever-widening avenues of experience and power. It is this actual state of affairs that places an arrest on the detractors of humanism. We do begin not with a theory, or even with a truth, but with the imposing need of establishing our personal reality through our answerability to such men as we may meet.

We may not turn aside from the moment or, in the name of a theory, dismiss those we encounter. If free societies have a quarrel with despotisms, this is the core of the issue. One cannot call one's soul one's own if one cannot call the moment one's own. Democracy has no ideology. It has no orthodoxy. Nor has history such an orthodoxy. The moment is all; the readiness is all. Respect for experience has gone too far with us to be recalled. At bottom it is respect for persons.

35

Reflections and Aphorisms

i. A Short Outline

The story seems to be this:

(1) The emergence of the individual.

(2) The separatistic and nonsocial status of that new individual (skepticism, sophistry, cynicism, hedonism, nominalism).

(3) Alliance with the universe (stoicism), but no local and actual alliance with persons or institutions.

(4) The reaffirmation of the individual in Christianity; suggestion of an essential community in the doctrine of charity; "the communion of Saints," this communion not inherent and constitutive of the individual, but operative through the circuit of a divine love; alliance via the otherworldly; the Church as authoritarian moralist for centuries; a moral universe; the dubious status of local control (Calvin, Edwards).

(5) The gradual displacement of a moral universe by a scientific universe.

(6) The absorption of the individual into the scientific universe (the nervous "system," "stimulus-response" psychology); "behavioral science"; a scientific psychology and the denial of local control—as in physics, the master science; any local control a superstition, any actuality a "myth"; "theories" of history in terms of the ahistoric; the disparagement of emotion; nonindividuating art; the new

search for a vanishing "identity" as a revolt from the loss of the individual.

(7) The constitutional status of the act; primal local control as generator of all universals; the actual as noncognitive but the source of all cognition.

But this new account of alliance can appear only as the earlier individual has been quite lost. It is *not* an attempt to make that early supposed individual social. Its force derives from the very authority of the new scientific world that has displaced the moral universe. It is the need of preserving the scientific world itself. It is the claim that space, time, and quantity derive from *verbs,* from measuring, telling time, calculating in numbers. It claims an ontological status for the *functioning object,* for yardsticks, clocks, numbers, words, for *the* body, which is identified only in functioning and as local control, and from which, along with all functioning objects, a world is entailed and projected. It establishes a midworld—utterances—as the basis for the very distinction between subject and object, a distinction that otherwise has no basis, and never had a basis.

ii. Consequences

It is at the point where consequences get taken into account—where one first sees that there *are* consequences, that they are one's own, that action is what produces them and *alone* produces them—that one becomes moral. In history one seeks the extension, but never the transcendence, of the moment.

iii. Error

The historical is the only area in which error finds objectification. This is a matter of first importance, since any view of knowledge that leaves error in the mind will have its truth in no other place. We *make* mistakes; we don't think mistakes. And they are there for everyone to see, provided one looks for them in the artifacts and gives up at last the mystique of the facts that is the dogmatist's delight and the skeptic's opportunity. In history we not only consort with error and evil; we actually make them, objectify them, enshrine them in institutions, glorify them with rite and ceremony, and die for them. What a bloodless view of truth it is that does not include error in the same processes by which it itself is born. It used to be said that the truth was mysterious and perhaps beyond our powers. We are, however, in no less peril when error, and the great and calamitous errors, are relegated to nonsense, underived, and made into "pseudo-concepts." One may count on it that to avoid error is to avoid history, and to have no constitutional place for error is to leave the historical undefined and the dateless truth a monstrous arbitrariness.

iv. To Omit Artifacts Is to Omit History

History, dealing in the past tense, finds its materials only in created objects. Any theory of knowledge which omits artifacts omits history and will result in telling us what is so, but not in telling what was done.

v. The Trouble with a Static Rule

The trouble with a static rule is not that it is false, or that another one would be better, but that one cannot do what such a rule says. Agency is responsibility—and therefore one's own—only as it becomes the continuum of an articulate utterance. The fortunes of action in the present tense are clear: there is no such act. The result of a frozen moralism is that one can do nothing. Those who propose such rules do not want anyone to act. Action is to be under the law rather than the source of law in its self-maintenance. Mechanism and behaviorism are no more than the transference to objects of the same static account of action that was long the prerogative of the static subject. This controversy has now ended in the exhaustion of both contestants.

vi. Order Is Nonterminating

Order is nonterminating both within itself and in its recognized form. There is more afoot than purposes that seek specific ends and then come to a full stop. Schopenhauer thought that life was a mistake because its activities resulted from desires and irritations that, when sated, were followed by a stupid lethargy. Accidental and terminating enterprises have no history. But some concerns appear interminable and feed on themselves rather than on casual attraction or repulsion. The historical excludes the complete, whether as perfection or as having been finished or as capable of being finished. There are many histories, and all occur apropos of continuing organizations—science, the arts, economics, philosophy, the state. In these everyone shares, not deliberately, but actually. All of them have a past, and none is to be understood in the present tense alone. All are dated actualities, not realities.

Changes have occurred not only in content but also in form—that is, in the structure and control of utterance. Psychology, for example, no longer construes action as deliberate, calculated to effect a specific result or to exemplify a prior ideal. After Darwin nonrational controls appeared. That way of accounting for acts was found inadequate by instinct theory, and instinct has itself been modified by the psychology of the unconscious, a decidedly different orientation—different in both stimulus and response—from the process of learning about, or dealing with, objects of nature. The modern political society rests on the idea of "rights," essentially a demand for the recognition of spontaneous energies as the condition of community. This is not an idea found in Plato's *Republic*, where the emphasis is on an eternal justice "whether seen or unseen by gods or by men." Nor is it the community of the Old or New Testament. There is history only where there is order, but only where order itself has been modified and the change marked by a date.

The incomplete—without which there is no history or articulate order—has been neglected as a constitutional idea, with vast consequences for character and thought. To share in the incomplete is to be in history.

vii. Mutuality and Independence

Morality is the association with history—that is, with the revisionary. But it is also supposed that morality is in the tribal mores, in the static folkways and customs. Either way, there is the need of being like others. What sort of "being like others" is one to adopt? It must be some way that leaves one also independent. This is the argument for free institutions. They claim to be the vehicle of the moral because they are the locus of the self-directing, promising some sort of life not wholly dictated by nature, the supernatural, or society. On the other hand morality requires also the acceptance of a person for what he now is; it requires the affections.

"Join others" is not enough; "obey the law" is not enough to define—or to recommend—morality. Recognition, however, is not to be had in the tribal. There, one is like another. Nor is it to be had in the independent and separate. One needs a way of combining the independent with the mutual. The mutuality that is also the recognition of the independent is in the joining of forces in the effectiveness of action—that is, in the acts that make a difference to action itself. One needs the ease and security of the tribal, but also the personal reality of the independent.

We can make history only where we are identified with ways that we can love and adopt, but that we can so love and adopt only because they suggest and embody their own revision and clarification. So one loves and adopts a science, or a society that can be articulated in art, or a policy that promises its own fulfillment as it avoids the destruction inherent in its defects.

viii. Disclosure

History is not "about" a past; it is the disclosure and vehicle of the past. Except as a career and a continuum there is no past to write "about." And if a career, then the present has joined and embraced its past.

ix. The Past Is Not Come Upon

We do not come upon a past as upon something new, extraneous, or merely additional. To inherit one's mother tongue is to have spoken and to have heard, to have been addressed by and to have attended to others. Something of the past has already become part of one's activities. No one begins a lively acquaintance with objects or persons by studying history. One learns first to conduct oneself in ways that only later on disclose their historical implications.

x. The Price of the Actual

The actual exacts a high price, and it has nothing to offer but itself. If one is not willing to be defined in one's actuality, one reverts to disorder or to the timeless. But to say that is not to make an argument; it is only to note what the nonhistorical and the ahistoric have actually revealed. Here there is no peculiar or unique feature of self-identification. There is no argument for disorder, any more than for an invariant formality. Both appear as essays in self-discovery. Neither appears as an unreflective fact or as a datum of a passive perception. The objectification of time is itself a stage of self-discovery—that is, of history.

xi. Time and the Humanities

What is at stake in the bearing of time on our identities is not only the materials of history books. It is rather all of the humanities and, indeed, all modes of learning in which there is nothing to be known apart from the telling.

xii. The Price of the Past

The price of a historical past is a historical present. Where there is a fixed past, it is in the interest of a fixed present, so that one "is" of a certain race or creed or nation, not that one could become so, nor that the past was also a becoming in its own time and place.

xiii. Success

Anyone with a past has failed and succeeded in at least some of the ways in which it is possible to do so. It would not be possible to say what those ways might be had success and failure not marked them out for our notice.

xiv. Precedents

A rule without antecedents or liability to revision lacks, in the end, any relevance or meaning, since it could never be elucidated in words, which are themselves the vehicles of accumulated experience. Such a rule, purporting to be independent of history, operates only as a natural force and can be met only by force. Indeed, the usual interpretation of a breach of an ahistoric moral rule places the violator in as arbitrary a position as the rule itself. The trouble with crime is not that it manifests a disregard of an ahistoric natural law, but rather that it can generate no precedents. The lawyers have the precedents, and that is why they are the interpreters of the law. The decision that "stands" invokes the processes by which it had been derived and through which its present meaning will undergo modification. Every word is regulative, and every law takes time to become intelligible.

xv. Law, Physical and Moral

The need for law, whether physical or moral, is constitutional, not episodic or accidental. It is law that makes an immediacy possible. Law does not externally regulate the identifiable datum; it is rather a condition of its discovery. The historic distinction of Kant's ethical proposals rests on his assimilation of personal identity with the social bond.

It was a constitutional question and for that reason escaped the observation of utilitarian moralists, and won rejection by authoritarians. The unself-conscious always view the imperatives of actuality as a defect of intelligence because imperatives are not produced by the intelligence.

The sense of history became systematic as a reaction to the equally systematic impersonality of the ahistoric ideal. That is why history is an "idea," a constitutional factor of experience. It took time to discover history as no less philosophical than the static categories of Aristotle or Kant. The necessary remained arbitrary, or a mere postulate, until it had been derived. Since no category is derived from the accidental, it springs authoritatively only from a constitutional inadequacy. And that takes time—not the dateless time of physics, but the dated and unique time of history.

xvi. Institutions

In all institutions there is a claim to control, to knowledge of truth and of values. One may allege of institutions that they are as ill-founded as private opinion or desire, but what one cannot allege is that they have become actual when men have entertained a belief in their own nonentity. Church, state, and private order proclaim a conviction of man's alliance with truths and values that control his vagrancies and inspire his efforts. They involve rejections and exclusive affirmations. They stand for the belief that not anything will do, that some opinions and directions will not do. They bind the endeavors made in time and finitude to eternal truths and values.

xvii. A Common Past

It is roughly the case that present-day unity among men is likewise the unity of their common past. We are most congenial with those peoples whose development has involved them in our problems, or with those whose past is our past. This is more than a psychological similarity.

Considerable differences in personal tastes and habits prevail within close societies. But these may not be serious if the grounds of appeal to criticism are common. It is worth a great deal to disputants to find common ground in the problems of Moses, Plato, Paul, Newton, Luther, Blackstone, or Jefferson. Appeal can be taken to those acknowledged modes of defining the meaning of an issue and the criteria of a solution. Where nations or persons face a diverse past, they can give proportionately smaller guarantee for a common future. They will not mean the same by the words through which social order is maintained. Russians speak of democracy but do not mean at all what we mean. For us democracy means the law that gives scope to privacy of will; to them privacy of will is the root of all evil.

xviii. Philosophy

To view history philosophically is to consider it as a constitutional mode of experience, a way of organization no less fundamental than physics or logic.

xix. Superstition

Nobody prefers opinion to knowledge, or superstition to truth. There is no reason to suppose that Noah in offering a burnt sacrifice after safely coming through the flood had any doubt that he was thereby establishing rapport with the power controlling man and nature, putting himself right with that power in a fashion to affect his own security and well-being. Burnt offerings are no longer made, but it seems neither accurate nor generous to suppose that later methods of control have quite different motives.

xx. The Transcendental

Those who live in the eternal can do nothing for its own sake—neither play nor work, neither manual nor intellectual labor. There is something trivializing in this inability to love or hate thoroughly. Then no poem is for its own sake, but must celebrate something else, something remote. Within time there can then be no abandonment and nothing innocent, except what is done in ignorance of man and of nature, an ignorance of every experience that sets a world before one. Any such vision must be renounced in favor of an eternal hope or a transcendent reality.

In consequence, the most profound of all schisms takes place in the personality as the temporal becomes opposed to the eternal. One becomes incapable of action. There remain to one pseudo-acts, which are sin. In sober moments one repudiates them as not expressive of one's true will, but only of some earthly and fleshly desires, of the natural man, who is never the essential man. What one desires or can discover can never become the basis of a world, but remains in the end irrelevant to the universal and infinite. The natural man, his desires and experiences, is doomed to disorder and darkness. What he has to be concerned with is his soul, and that is neither defined nor satisfied in terms of nature, according to the transcendentalist view.

But history, the reality of time, can have no serious authority where time itself is unreal. All the efforts made to secure the reality of time are themselves useless, mistaken, and wicked. The making of history becomes in principle impious in any outlook that regards time as the pensioner of the timeless. Businessmen, politicians, and scholars are then only boys who busy themselves with concerns of lesser moment. Activity of that sort may keep us out of the mischief that idleness invents. But men who take such activities seriously display only a brutish dullness to "higher" or "spiritual" values. The more mundane our concerns, the more obvious becomes the contrast with transcendental guidance.

xxi. What Is to Be Done about the Pilgrims?

There is nothing practical to be done about the landing of the Pilgrims. What one does about the past reflects will, not purpose. That there were Pilgrims at all appears to some as an apostasy, to others an emancipation, to no one a way of proposing or executing a present purpose.

xxii. Physics Has a History

In 1581 Galileo observed the equal periods in the swing of a suspended lamp in the cathedral at Pisa. That he saw it speaks for the man he was, and what he did about his observation is part of the history of physics, but the laws of the pendulum are not abrogated in Padua or in Poona. Viewed as physics, the knowledge could have been acquired in Florence, or in some other year, or by another man. But Galileo is in history, and he is there because he gave distinction to the year 1581.

xxiii. Economic Determination

The economic determination of history would require that economics be left a wholly free and spontaneous activity, so that "history" would be its resultant. As soon as the economic order is in any way controlled, the aim is non-economic and the consequences are noneconomic. It may be true that he who controls economics controls social and political forms also. That is the case. Tell a man what he must do or what he may do, set any restriction on what he may do or on what he receives, and one thereby controls social and political hierarchy.

But the control of economics does not prove that history is controlled by economics; it proves, rather, that it is determined by something else.

The idea that history can be controlled at all is the sign that history is not thought fundamental. The control of history is tyranny. It is in any form—atheistic or theistic—dogmatic and repressive. Economics must itself appear in history: emerge, develop, and change in a free medium.

xxiv. Outside and Inside

Collingwood thinks that history studies the "inside" of events; physics, the outside.

But do events have an "inside"? Is there action, or only reaction? Many would deny the inside. All who assert the origin of knowledge in lawfully changing objects deny the inside.

History is not concerned with anything so mysterious as an inside. What, one may ask, is the situation which is neither out nor in, in terms of which the distinction is made? Is the outside to be ascertained without an inside? What is their relation, the basis of their distinction? For it requires some basis. How, for that matter, does one come to an *out*side? That has been itself a contested point. Some say one cannot do it. Some say that there is neither out nor in, but only phenomena, data, sense qualities, appearances.

The historical cannot be subsequent to this distinction, so that one says that history deals with an inside already known as opposed to an outside already known. The distinction must itself be tinged with the time sense, must be a product of the clarification of thought and central to the meaning of thought.

This distinction occurs through the symbol and the artifact. Here the difference is reconciled, subject and object being here inseparable. The *objectified act* is the basis of all objectivity and all subjectivity too. The subjective is, in principle, what leaves no objective memorial yet can be understood only by appeal to such memorials.

xxv. Criticism and History

Men respect force—that is, what can arrest what they are already doing. Nobody pays attention to ideas unless he already acts through them and so sees his action arrested if the ideas he holds seem confused. History is a form of arrest—that is, of criticism. Our ways of acting become challenged. Not all societies do as ours do; so not all persons feel (art), think (science), or associate (morals) as we do. So there is alienation from others and hence loss of power and a threat to oneself. In so far as one's own power is based on an idea, mere violence or mere disregard of others does not make for smooth operation. An idea can win only on its own ground, by succeeding as idea. Hence one needs ideas that can appropriate other ideas and so can continue to operate in the face of opposition. These are the ideas of organization, of societies, of modes of apprehension of nature, of views of man as a person. Thus we meet forces that are systematic, not only episodic. History is the criticism of the systematic. It is the force of arrest in what is systematic in oneself. It is, therefore, the disclosure that one has systematic ideas but that these are actual and practical and moral, not subjective, not cerebral, but capable of challenge through action and its frustration.

xxvi. Passing Judgment

The great seduction of philosophy is to pass judgment and so to be right. To be right puts one above confusions and suggests that in some essential respect one has escaped from vulnerability. Most of us would rather be right than be in history. We do not, indeed, know where we would be if we were not right, unless we were to be wrong. So we claim to be right. But in history one passes no edicts of excommunication, and that does not fit our orthodoxy.

xxvii. History Does Not Excommunicate

If the Eleatics too are in history, then they spoke for their time, thereby creating a past and purchasing their own historicity at the price of their modification. And so, if one speaks of them in the historical temper, it is not to overthrow or to excommunicate, but to bring them into the continuum of our living heritage.

xxviii. Anachronism

The besetting fallacy of history is anachronism, the description of any past in terms of an abstract present. History writing that is not the imaginative reconstruction of a past on its own terms, indeed the very discovery of such terms, leaves the past as a mystery or else reduces it to the ahistoricity of scientific nature, to psychological atomism or theological incomprehension.

xxix. Symbols and Tongues

The past cannot address one in one's own language. One must learn the language of the past. It is not accommodating or kind, and can't be ordered to make itself clear to one.

We go to it because our own language is unclear to us, containing words and institutions that may seem meaningless, superstitious, useless, ignorant. But neither are we quite free of such words. They come into our own speech and into that of our neighbors. They need attention for our own sakes. The alternative is a return to ignorance. It is a return not to nature, but to the uncouth and animal life. We are in league with meanings in ourselves that our own experience has not produced. We do not, therefore, know what our words mean unless we search out those experiences of others by which they have come to mean what they now mean to us.

Were all our own words clear, the need of this search would not occur. But our words come from many minds and outlooks. Our heritage is a mess and is full of confusion. We inherit a confusion of symbols and a confusion of tongues.

In what sort of words and symbols is this confusion the source of history? Not in common nouns. A "porch" is also a "stoop"; a "fried cake," a "doughnut"; a ton, 2,000 pounds or 2,240 pounds. We ask, "How do you use a word for an agreed-upon object?" It is when nobody can answer that question that we turn to history. It is where words lack clear meaning to whoever uses them, where words are purely intentional and not denotational. It is such words that carry the historical dimension.

xxx. Change

Ordinarily change is measured with reference to the permanent and is explained in terms of the permanent. Thus a change in the weather gets explained by reference to the unchanging laws of air masses, or a change in the velocity of an auto by reference to the gradient, the amount of gas fed into cylinders, and the like. But historical change involves one in the paradox of attempting to understand the discontinuous. It seems plain that if there were no discontinuous change there could be no historical knowledge as an independent sort of knowledge. For so-called historical changes would then be merely special cases of change of some other sort. The accepted types of change are few in number, probably only change in physics and change in psychology. Perhaps psychology itself falls back into physics. At any rate, one shrinks from finding in history nothing more than a rather inexpert form of physics.

xxxi. One Point of View

There can be only one point of view from which history can be written, and further, there is such a point of view. Obviously something of this sort is necessary if history is to avoid dogmatic assertions of what really happened or skeptical refusal to say what really happened. Whatever the one point of view may be through which history needs to be written if it is to escape subjectivity, it seems that it, too, is a historical resultant. Thus the one necessary point of view from which history is to be written is itself the outcome of history.

xxxii. Our Heritage

The present is no Olympian height from which all history is to be judged as from some timeless perspective. We are the heirs not only of past wealth, but also of past debits.

xxxiii. Caesar Is Not Crossing the Rubicon

It is not the case now that Caesar is crossing the Rubicon, or that Thomas Jefferson is writing the Declaration of Independence. These things are no more. Hence, a problem: What is it that is now true, yet can secure evidence only through a past that no longer is actual? In physics there is no analogue of this situation. If one says that water boils at 212° F., one means that some actually present water will boil at that temperature or, in some cases, is boiling at that temperature. There must be cases of present boiling, observed or inferred.

xxxiv. Originality

Originality is not, in principle, to be understood in terms of circumstance. Emerson, for example, is not to be reduced to issues already present in his world.

Originality faces the world in terms of the absolute confrontation of the world by the self. Given such absolute confrontation, a man will address himself to such issues as lie about him. But, transport an Emerson to England or to our Far West; let him soak up this new world; and he will say quite different things, though in the same spirit. The free mind is not made free by virtue of some specific issue—say, puritanism. All that is necessary—all that is possible—is *some* systematic issue. Thereafter many themes can be developed in that vein.

What is free and original is necessarily not to be accounted for through a specific occasion. That occasion will always be there, but only as occasion, never as explanation. Originality quickly shows this by going beyond the occasion that served to propose its necessity. It confronts its occasion with no more partiality than it shows to any other systematic factor of experience. Originality is this general capacity for the perception of systematic factors.

Referring men to their times is sometimes done by people who see no originality in the times, either; puritanism gets treated as a deplorable lapse. Reaction to what is not itself free can produce no freedom. So I would suggest that it is only the articulation of freedom in the past of a man that can constitute the occasion of his own discovery of freedom. The influences operating on originality are always original.

When the union between the original mind and other original minds is perceived, one has responsibility. Such responsibility is clearly perceived only by the mind that is *first* original and, like Emerson, a fellow of *all* original minds.

One can't get into history until one stands outside of circumstance.

xxxv. Motives and Reactions

Consider such claims as these: (1) British propaganda took us into the First World War. (2) Economic motives controlled the Constitution.

Here what was done is the result of forces acting on people. The forces *look* psychic, but the manner of their operation is analogous to that of physical forces. Here is the man, and there is the force. The force controls the man.

Is such talk historical at all? I think not. It never really tells what anybody did, but only what was brought about.

Such views can only indicate what forces were operating. Economic forces operated to keep the Puritan clergy from feeling popular sympathy. They likewise operated to make sure the British won the First World War so that Morgan could secure his loans. They operated to bring about the French Revolution. This is like saying that hot air masses, plus the rotation of the earth, are forces contributing to the formation and behavior of Hurricane Carol, and of Edna, and of Hazel.

What is the alternative? The alternative is not to look for other and better or truer motives. That would not change the picture in principle.

I suggest that what one needs to look for in finding out controls of events is not anybody's motives, but what events or statements determined an act. For example, it seems that much enthusiasm for Eisenhower was aroused in 1952 because he said he would go to Korea. The connection between his going and the final armistice is not clear. Preliminary negotiations had already gone far. But going to Korea was done to put an end to the war. This is what people wanted. They wanted to be sure that the president knew all about Korea, and that a resolute and informed diplomacy would put an end to supposed drift.

This seems to me not an assertion of hidden motives and controls, but a statement of what happened in terms of a *reaction* to a specific situation. MacArthur never wanted to leave Korea, and he claimed to know all about it, too. But when it came to votes at the convention, he did poorly.

I would propose that the action with which one deals in history is always a reaction. We reacted to Pearl Harbor. Perhaps no one knows all the factors of temper in that reaction. Nor could one say in advance of the reaction that Americans don't like to be shot at. Maybe they don't mind. One never knows apart from what is done at a time and place.

Historical action does not, I would say, operate in terms of what men antecedently are. It operates in the disclosure of what they are in those reactions that serve to focus major energies. That is why history takes reaction seriously. There would be no reason to do so if there were ahistoric ways of finding out whether people loved money or peace. History then would be unnecessary.

Science understands the particular only via the universal. History has no antecedent universals. It is the true empiricism.

xxxvi. Cyclic Theories

Taken literally, the doctrine of the return implies a finite universe—one, that is, in which all possible changes have taken place. An infinite universe, capable of endless combination, *need* not repeat. A finite universe *must* repeat and cannot go on with novelties forever.

In a hypothetically finite situation no repetition could be discovered, since not all the components could be taken into account.

xxxvii. Presence

It has become orthodox to deny that a person is present in his errors and his crimes. By the same token, no one is present in his truth or his virtue.

xxxviii. Nihilism

Of course our current nihilism is itself a historical emergence. It was not original. It should be seen as history, not truth. I would propose as a test for the historian that he identify some fatality in the *present,* a present confusion and conflict brought on by the articulate past. To be in history is to see the present as a historical fate, not as above or outside the momentum of the actual. So I say that the current hostility to the generative power of the act is not without a basis. But I assert that this basis is not a "truth" that surveys acts and therefore sees act as myth and illusion, but the struggle of the act to discover its own constituents. Truth proposed as a fixity has come under attack, and this because it nullifies the *process* by which fixity has itself been generated. But as rebels from fixity we then fly to its antithesis and embrace Calibanism.

xxxix. Good in History

History does not show men good or bad; it operates by assuming that they are moral—that is, agents. Good, in history, can mean only the perpetuation of those critical processes that define the moral.